RooseveltCare

How Social Security Is Sabotaging
the Land of Self-Reliance

Don Watkins

AYN RAND
INSTITUTE PRESS

First Printing 2014

ISBN: 978-0-9794661-7-5

AynRand.org

CONTENTS

*For Olivia Watkins, in the hopes that your generation
will not be forced to pay the debts of mine,
and Alex Epstein, for showing the way.*

ACKNOWLEDGMENTS

I am grateful, above all, for the support of the Ayn Rand Institute and its supporters for making this project (and all my projects) possible. For their generous editorial assistance, I would like to thank Yaron Brook, Eric Daniels, Adam Edmonsond, Alex Epstein, Onkar Ghate, and especially Thomas Bowden, who edited several early drafts of the manuscript and did much to improve it. I am also indebted to Kate Watkins, Rebecca Bernbach, Elan Journo, Amanda Maxham, Donna Montrezza, Simon Federman, Leonard Peikoff, Gregory Salmieri, Steve Simpson, Peter Schwartz, Richard Salsman, Chad Morris, Lin Zinser, and Richard Ralston for their varied forms of support.

INTRODUCTION

Just over a year ago, as I was beginning to write this book, my wife and I had our first child. Olivia was born into the world with two loving parents, four doting grandparents—and a share of government debt amounting to hundreds of thousands of dollars thanks mainly to our ravenous entitlement state.[1]

Today we are at a crossroads. America's entitlement state is threatening to bankrupt us, and new schemes such as ObamaCare are hastening the collapse. The numbers are terrifying. Owing primarily to Social Security, Medicare, and Medicaid, the U.S. government's true debt amounts to more than $200 *trillion* dollars according to some economists.[2]

The government has made promises in our name that we have no way to keep, and any attempt to *try* to keep them will mean robbing my generation and my daughter's generation of many of our hopes and dreams. The best estimates suggest that Olivia will have to pay roughly $400,000 more in taxes than she will ever receive in handouts—in order to provide her grandparents' generation with handouts that are $300,000 greater than they paid in taxes.[3]

To make up this $200 trillion shortfall, *all* federal taxes would have to rise by 54.8 percent immediately and forever. If tax rates aren't raised for twenty years, that number skyrockets to 65.3 percent. And all of these projections assume that interest rates remain low. But as our debt rises, so does the likelihood that interest rates will balloon. If that happens, it's game over.

I call this Welfaregate. It is the scandal of our time, and if we don't change course, then at some point in the not-too-distant future, we're going to face a day of reckoning. But what should we do? While Washington evades the whole issue, a growing number of commentators have started sounding the alarm. While they deserve our gratitude for shining a light on this problem, their proposed solutions are usually built on the assumption that the entitlement state is a moral institution that we must save.

But what if it's not?

My interest in the entitlement state started when, at the age of seventeen, I was told that my generation would never see a dime of Social Security. Having recently landed my first job as an usher at the local movie theater, I knew just how many dimes were being taken out of my paycheck to pay for Social Security. Why, I wondered, was I being forced to pay for a program that wouldn't be around when it was my turn to retire? Where was my money going? And why in the world couldn't I opt out of the program and plan for my future the way I wanted? After all, it was my money, right?

I quickly learned that my skepticism was unusual. Social Security is one of the government's most popular programs: Eight out of ten Americans believe "Social Security has been good for the country," according to a 2011 CNN/ORC International poll.[4] How could it not have been? We have been taught that, in those dark days before Social Security, elderly Americans lived in terror of losing their jobs, knowing that it would mean the poorhouse if not outright starvation. Social Security changed that. It made America a more humane, more secure, more prosperous nation. So the story went.

Even as a kid, I did not think that settled the issue. Sure, I thought, America may have been a rough place to live before Social Security, but we had come a long way since 1935. We now lived in a nation where even most poor people owned cars and TVs, and had plenty to eat. Why would we structure our political and economic system around a fear that properly belonged to the nineteenth century, not the twenty-first?

When I revisited this issue as an adult, however, I discovered something that left me truly astonished. When I looked into the history of America before Social Security and the circumstances that led to the creation of the entitlement state, what I found was the exact opposite of everything I had ever been taught. In many ways, America was a *better* place to live before the creation of Social Security—and Social Security played a key role in making America worse.

I had known America was much freer before the entitlement state. Americans took the Declaration of Independence seriously. The government played the important role of protecting us from criminals and foreign threats, but otherwise left us pretty much alone. Each individual could pursue his own happiness, using his property to build for himself the kind of life he chose. What I didn't know was how well most Americans fared in that setting. Even at a time when capitalism had only started to lift people out of poverty, the vast, vast majority of men and women in this country were able to cope with life's challenges, supporting themselves and their families through productive work, and carving out an existence that was richer and more fulfilling than anywhere else on the globe.

Even more striking, though, was the moral stature of those Americans. This was a land of giants: men and women who displayed a scale of self-esteem and unbounded benevolence that is hard to imagine in our cynical times. There was a deep well of enthusiasm for life that sprang from a conviction that they were creating a better, brighter world. It was a world where all could prosper—and prosperity came not at the expense of other people but through one's own hard work and creative effort. In a word, it was a magnificent culture of *self-reliance*.

By the time of the passage of Social Security in 1935, that culture was at the beginning of its end. Although American self-reliance has not completely vanished in the decades since Franklin D. Roosevelt created the entitlement state, it is ebbing. Here's one small but telling example. An earlier America had held up the self-made man as an ideal to strive for—the Andrew Carnegie type who pulls himself up "by his own bootstraps" and rises "from rags to riches."

Today, in our allegedly more sophisticated age, we have been taught that economic mobility is a myth, Horatio Alger stories are a delusion, and the ideal we should aim for is not the life of Andrew Carnegie but the "Life of Julia," a fictional character cooked up by the Obama administration in early 2012 to illustrate how success is made possible only by the beneficent hand of a government entitlement system that coddles us from cradle to grave.[5]

As we prepare to decide the fate of entitlements, we need to revisit the story of the entitlement state, and above all the story of Social Security. Social Security is not just another government spending program. Historically, the passage of the Social Security Act in 1935 marked the birth of the American entitlement state. Economically, it is the most expensive program in the government's budget. Legally, most of our federal entitlement programs are included under the Social Security Act and its amendments. These include:

- Survivors Insurance
- Disability Insurance
- Unemployment benefits
- Temporary Assistance for Needy Families ("welfare")
- Health Insurance for Aged and Disabled (Medicare)
- Grants to States for Medical Assistance Programs (Medicaid)
- State Children's Health Insurance Program (SCHIP)

- Supplemental Security Income (SSI)
- Patient Protection and Affordable Care Act ("ObamaCare")

We've been taught that the program has played a profoundly positive role in fulfilling the promise of America, correcting disturbing shortcomings in our capitalist system. It's time this myth be put to rest and replaced with the truth: Social Security is an *un-American* program that is helping to transform us from a self-reliant society into an entitlement society, and causing us to lose much of what was great about this country:

- The self-reliant society celebrated the fact that you could better yourself by creating wealth. The entitlement society is based on the notion that you are basically helpless unless society provides you with wealth and opportunity wrestled from others.
- The self-reliant society had a profound respect for the individual and his property. The entitlement society regards individuals and their property as means to society's ends.
- The self-reliant society was based on the conviction that there is a harmony of interests among men, who therefore can live together voluntarily. The entitlement society regards conflicts of interest as inherent in human relationships, thereby unleashing a dog-eat-dog war of all against all.
- The self-reliant society protected and encouraged the independent individual, who rationally planned and governed his own life. The entitlement society caters to the chronically passive slacker who would rather not be burdened with such a profound responsibility.
- The self-reliant society gave us Andrew Carnegie, Thomas Edison, and Ben Franklin. The entitlement society gave us Julia, Octomom, and Barack Obama.

This is not another book for policy wonks about the financial trouble Social Security is in. You will find no graphs or complicated accounting concepts in the pages ahead. This is the story of the role that Social Security and the entitlement state have played in eroding the eagerness, energy, and optimism that once defined this country.

It is also a guide for fighting back. A solution to today's crisis is possible, but it will not come from our political leaders willing to do no more than tinker with benefit formulas. It will have to come from individual Americans who are willing to say: I am not my grandfather's keeper.

To create just such a movement I launched a campaign to end the debt draft—that is, to abolish the entitlement programs that have conscripted young Americans into serving the needs of the elderly rather than pursuing their own happiness. I have included our manifesto as an appendix. To learn more about this campaign, you can visit our website at www.endthedebtdraft.com.

I do not choose to be a common man. It is my right to be uncommon—if I can. I seek opportunity—not security. I do not wish to be a kept citizen, humbled and dulled by having the state look after me. I want to take the calculated risk; to dream and to build, to fail and to succeed. I refuse to barter incentive for a dole. . . . I will not trade freedom for beneficence nor my dignity for a handout. I will never cower before any master nor bend to any threat. It is my heritage to stand erect, proud and unafraid; to think and act for myself, enjoy the benefit of my creations, and to face the world boldly and say, this I have done. This is what it means to be an American.[6]

—Dean Alfange

CHAPTER ONE

Before Social Security (1776–1934)

Here is the myth: Social Security is a quintessentially American program that rescued millions from destitution and laid the foundation for a more moral society. The truth is that Social Security marked the abandonment of the American ideal of self-reliance. The results have been devastating.

The Self-Reliant Society

America was born out of the Enlightenment, a philosophical, cultural, and political epoch in which people embraced the view of the individual human being as a rational creature, who has the ability and the right to live according to his own independent judgment, for the sake of his own success and happiness. Its leitmotif was *self-esteem*—the individual of upright posture and fierce independence, who eagerly faces life's challenges and views others not as pawns or masters but as sovereign equals.[7]

This outlook bred a profound respect for limited government, free markets, and private property that ran deep in the American psyche, finding its ultimate expression in the Founding Fathers, whose project was to limit government in order to liberate the individual. The "sum of good government," said Jefferson, is

> a wise and frugal Government, which shall restrain men from injuring one another, shall leave them otherwise free to regulate their own pursuits of industry and improvement, and shall not take from the mouth of labor the bread it has earned.[8]

What emerged from this foundation was the social system we now call capitalism—a system in which the government guarded individual rights, including property rights, and left the economy free. In

Ralph Waldo Emerson's words:

> The basis of political economy is non-interference. The
> only safe rule is found in the self-adjusting meter of
> demand and supply. Do not legislate. Meddle, and you
> snap the sinews with your sumptuary laws. Give no boun-
> ties: make equal laws: secure life and property, and you
> need not give alms. Open the doors of opportunity to
> talent and virtue, and they will do themselves justice, and
> property will not be in bad hands. In a free and just com-
> monwealth, property rushes from the idle and imbecile, to
> the industrious, brave, and persevering.[9]

In Emerson's description we see a perspective that is all but alien
today, and yet was for a century and a half part of the American mind:
the conviction that the foundation of success is *character*. "Industry,
honesty, perseverance, sticking to one thing, invariably lead to success," wrote Matthew Hale Smith in 1873.[10]

The central virtue, the one that made all of these others possible,
was what Emerson called "the sublimity of Self-reliance." Although
seldom defined with total clarity, self-reliance generally referred to an
individual's commitment to assume the responsibility of building a
life for himself by dint of his own independent thought and productive effort. It did not mean that one spurned others. A self-reliant man
learned from others, worked with others, befriended others—but he
was not dependent on them for his livelihood. He did not view his life
as other people's responsibility. He pulled his own weight.

If morality means a commitment to the virtues and values that
foster human life, then the self-reliant man was eminently moral.
Self-reliance made one upright in character and eager to act. Man
was not controlled by "fate" or his parents or society. Even the poorest American, it was believed, could make something of himself if
he took responsibility for improving his lot. "Of all the elements of
success," counseled a popular success guide from 1888,

> none is more essential than self-reliance, —determination
> to be one's own helper, and not to look for others for sup-
> port. . . . No man can gain true success, no matter how
> situated, unless he depends upon no one but himself;
> remember that.[11]

In his enormously popular rags-to-riches tales, written in the second half of the nineteenth century, Horatio Alger became perhaps the greatest voice for the ideal of self-reliance. Alger once said that the goal of his work was to "stimulate the ambition of those boys who are hampered by poverty and limited advantages, and teach them that an honorable position in life may be attained by those who are willing to work for it."[12] Your external circumstances may not be conducive to success, but in a free country, your own choices and actions determined your future. You could write your own story.

The American ideal of self-reliance implied that to be a good person was to take responsibility for your own life and to work to make something of it. It thus elevated the place of productive work in human life. Self-reliance amounted to the conviction that the world doesn't owe you a living, and so devoting your life to hard and diligent work is the foundation of a moral life and a moral society.

Historically, particularly in Europe, the earthly ideal most societies aspired to was a life of leisure—not relaxation from a hard day's work, which the self-reliant society would provide in abundance, but a life free from work.[13] America was different. Even before the American Revolution, visitors to the New World "were stunned by the numbers of Americans whose 'whole thoughts' were 'turned upon profit and gain.'"[14] In *Letters from an American Farmer*, written during the American Revolution, French American J. Hector St. John de Crèvecœur explains that

> we are all animated with the spirit of an industry which is unfettered and unrestrained, because each person works for himself. . . . Here the rewards of his industry follow with equal steps the progress of his labour; his labour is founded on the basis of nature, SELF-INTEREST: can it want a stronger allurement?[15]

By mid-nineteenth century, this focus on industry had been ingrained in the nation's soul. As one commentator notes:

> Almost without exception, visitors to the Northern states commented on the drawn faces and frantic busyness of Jacksonian Americans and complained of bolted meals, meager opportunities for amusement, and the universal preoccupation with what Charles Dickens damned as the "almighty dollar."[16]

It's hard today for us to understand just how central productive work was to American life during this country's first century and a half. People during that era showed up to cheer the launch of new bridges and trains the way Americans today greet the Super Bowl. Popular music celebrated technological achievements such as the telephone and the automobile. Daniel Yergin notes in his history of oil that during the late nineteenth century, "Americans danced to the 'American Petroleum Polka' and the 'Oil Fever Gallop,' and they sang such songs as 'Famous Oil Firms' and 'Oil on the Brain.'"[17]

Even the celebration of America's centennial in 1876 highlighted the nation's commercial achievements as much as its political achievements. At Machinery Hall in Philadelphia, "a profusion of mechanisms seduced the eye: power looms, lathes, sewing machines, presses, pumps, toolmaking machines, axles, shafts, wire cables, and locomotives."[18] The *Times of London* concluded that "The American invents as the Greek sculpted and the Italian painted: it is genius."[19]

Summarizing this phenomenon, Viennese immigrant Francis Grund concluded, after living in Boston for ten years:

> There is probably no people on earth with whom business constitutes pleasure, and industry amusement, in an equal degree with the inhabitants of the United States of America. Active occupation is not only the principal source of their happiness, and the foundation of their national greatness, but they are absolutely wretched without it, and . . . know but the horrors of idleness. Business is the very soul of an American: he pursues it, not as a means of procuring for himself and his family the necessary comforts of life, but as the fountain of all human felicity; . . . [I]t is as if all America were but one gigantic workshop, over the entrance of which there is the blazing inscription *"No admission here except on business."*[20]

This uniquely American attitude, with its unprecedented combination of self-interest, unbound benevolence, unflinching self-esteem, and enthusiasm for productive work, came from the same basic source. Under capitalism, *everyone could get better off at the same time,* each taking responsibility for his own life and prosperity.

In a self-reliant society, unlike aristocratic or tribal societies, people understood that they didn't have to fight over a relatively fixed amount of wealth. In America, they had both the freedom and the incentive to *create* vast amounts of new wealth for themselves. It was an environment that nurtured a profound and solemn sense of individual responsibility. Since no one could force others to support him, each man had to produce the wealth required for the support and enjoyment of his own life.

Of course individual responsibility is different from isolation, and when it came to dealing with other people, self-reliant Americans eagerly pursued their own interests *in concert* with others by means of each person's *voluntary* participation. They regularly found that it was advantageous to cooperate with others, leading Tocqueville to observe: "Americans of all ages, of all conditions, of all minds, constantly unite. . . . I often admired the infinite art with which the inhabitants of the United States succeeded in setting a common goal for the efforts of a great number of men, and in making them march freely toward it."[21] Self-reliant Americans worked together on the basis of mutual self-interest. There were families, communities, schools, tract societies, mechanics' societies, marine societies, societies for the promotion of industry, and much more.[22]

But the most distinctive social bond was *commerce*. As historian Gordon Wood observes, Americans "proudly and enthusiastically" viewed self-interest and money "as the best connecting links in society."[23] Samuel Blodget, writing in the early nineteenth century, called commerce and business the "*golden chains*" binding society together. "Commerce, that is, exchange, being in truth society itself, it is the only bond among men."[24] This was surely an overstatement, but Blodget was groping toward something true and profound: commerce—*making money*—was the moral foundation of American society. As Ayn Rand would explain the point in the twentieth century:

> To trade by means of money is the code of the men of good will. Money rests on the axiom that every man is the owner of his mind and his effort. Money allows no power to prescribe the value of your effort except the voluntary choice of the man who is willing to trade you his effort in return. Money permits you to obtain for your goods and your labor that which they are worth to the men who buy them, but no more. Money permits no deals except those to mutual benefit by the unforced judgment of the traders. Money demands of you the recognition that men must work for their own benefit, not for their own injury, for their gain, not their loss—the recognition that they

are not beasts of burden, born to carry the weight of your misery—that you must offer them values, not wounds—that the common bond among men is not the exchange of suffering, but the exchange of *goods*. . . . This is the code of existence whose tool and symbol is money.[25]

This was the essence of America before Social Security. Free individuals chose to support their lives through productive achievement, dealing with each other by means of mutually beneficial voluntary cooperation.

The glaring exception to this trend was the existence of slavery. Under slavery a man *wasn't* entitled to the product of his work. He wasn't free to pursue his own happiness: He was the servant of his master. He wasn't free to cooperate with others on voluntarily agreed upon terms. Slavery was the worst, most evil, most total form of compulsion. As Frederick Douglass explains, the slave

can own nothing, possess nothing, acquire nothing, but what must belong to another. To eat the fruit of his own toil, to clothe his person with the work of his own hands, is considered stealing. He toils that another may reap the fruit; he is industrious that another may live in idleness; he eats unbolted meal that another may eat the bread of fine flour.[26]

Slavery was the antithesis of the self-reliant society, individualism, property rights, and the work ethic—a vicious holdover from the pre-capitalist era. What its existence highlights is that self-reliance was an *ideal*—one that America did not always live up to in practice, and which ultimately led the nation to civil war.[27]

But it was the ideal of self-reliance and not the "right" to own slaves that formed the distinctively American spirit and drew millions of immigrants, who were eager to flock to this land of opportunity. They were drawn to promises not of security or the easy life but of *freedom* to pursue their own success and happiness. This 1850 poster calling for Irish immigrants was typical:

In the United States, labour is there the *first* condition of life, and industry is the lot of all men. Wealth is not idolized; but there is no degradation connected with labour; on the contrary, it is *honorable*, and held in general estimation.

In the remote parts of America, *an industrious youth* may follow any occupation without being looked down upon or sustain loss of character, and he may rationally expect to *raise himself* in the world by his labour.

In America, *a man's success* must altogether rest with himself—it will depend on his *industry, sobriety, diligence* and *virtue*; and if he do not succeed, in nine cases out of ten, the cause of the failure is to be found in the *deficiencies* of his own character.[28]

Not every American shared this attitude toward life, of course. No nation is filled only with the self-reliant and industrious, who seek nothing more than the right to live an independent existence. There were thieves, crooks, moochers, and bums—but the system was not designed for them. It was designed for the best among men and the best in each man. And just as subsidizing vice breeds vice, so a system geared toward virtue saw a blossoming of virtue.

There was perhaps no clearer illustration of this than the fact that the vast majority of Americans did not desire and often refused to accept the unearned. Government welfare "is an un-American thing," said the wife of an unemployed worker during the Great Depression. "It is a dole. No real person with a sense of responsibility wants" welfare.[29] Even among poor Americans, there was little call for redistributing wealth. Historian Gertrude Himmelfarb notes that the vast majority of workers during the nineteenth century

> believed that work, if not sacred, was essential not only to their sustenance but to their self-respect. They could, in fact, have had sustenance without work—in the poor-house, or on the dole, or from charity. But that would have put them in a condition of "dependency," which was repellent to the respectable working class, for it was precisely their "independence" that defined their "respectability."[30]

James Bryce, a keen observer of late-nineteenth-century American society, believed this was one of the reasons why Americans of his day were unwavering in their support for limited government and private property. They regarded these as moral imperatives.

> [T]he poorer citizens have long been a numerical majority, invested with political power. [And so we might fear] that the poor would have turned the tables on the rich, thrown the whole burden of taxation upon them, and disregarded in the supposed interest of the masses what are called the

rights of property. Not only has this not been attempted—
it has been scarcely even suggested . . . and it excites no
serious apprehension. There is nothing in the machinery
of government that could do more than delay it for a time,
did the masses desire it. What prevents it is the honesty and
common sense of the citizens generally, who are convinced
that the interests of all classes are substantially the same,
and that justice is the highest of those interests. Equality,
open competition, a fair field to everybody, every stimulus
to industry, and every security for its fruits, these they hold
to be the self-evident principles of national prosperity.[31]

In 1879, a shoe-cutter voiced similar sentiments, stressing that
it was not the poor but the *irresponsible* poor who were interested in
government handouts:

If working-people would drop the use of beer, tobacco,
and every thing else that is not of real benefit, and let such
men . . . earn their own living, they would have far more
money for the general expense of a family than they now
have. I live in a village of about two thousand inhabitants;
and I do not know of a family in destitute circumstances
which has let alone vicious expenditures, and been industrious. It is the idle, unthrifty, beer-drinking, don't-care
sort of people, who are out at the elbows, and waiting for
some sort of legislation to help them. The sooner working-people get rid of the idea that somebody or something
is going to help them, the better it will be for them. In
this country, as a general thing, every man has an equal
chance to rise. In our village there are a number of successful business men, and all began in the world without
any thing but their hands and a will to succeed. The best
way for working-people to get help is to help themselves.[32]

The root of these attitudes was the virtue of self-reliance.
American self-reliance, according to economist Nicholas Eberstadt,
meant that "in an environment bursting with opportunity, American
men and women viewed themselves as accountable for their own situation through their own achievements." As a result, they developed
"an affinity for personal enterprise and industry" along with

a horror of dependency and contempt for anything that
smacked of a mendicant mentality. Although many

Americans in earlier times were poor, even people in fairly desperate circumstances were known to refuse help or handouts as an affront to their dignity and independence.[33]

This was the state of American society in the era before the entitlement state. Whatever its flaws and failings, it was an essentially *moral* society, committed to freedom, self-reliance, and prosperity.

And prosperity is what it got.

The Invention of Prosperity

To grasp how enormous the economic achievements of the self-reliant society were, there is one error that we must not make: judging this era by modern standards. To condemn nineteenth-century capitalism because people worked longer and earned less than we do is no different than a twenty-second-century American bemoaning those poor twenty-first-century residents of Malibu because their cars didn't fly and they had to get by on only a few million dollars a year. To judge early American capitalism, we need to be mindful of historical context: What were living conditions like prior to the rise of the self-reliant society—and what were they like in societies of the time that didn't prize self-reliance?

Poverty is mankind's natural state. Undeveloped nature is not kind to human beings. It has to be transformed and developed if we're to survive at all, and it has to be transformed and developed on a massive scale if we're to thrive. For most of human history, development was minimal. The agricultural revolution made possible large-scale societies, but for thousands of years, little changed. Human beings created only a few basic tools and some primitive technologies. On the eve of industrial capitalism, life was brutal.

Here, for instance, is a description of life in Scotland for the typical seventeenth-century Scot:

> His lodging would sometimes have been in a hut of which every nook would have swarmed with vermin. He would have inhaled an atmosphere thick with peat smoke, and foul with a hundred noisome exhalations. . . . His couch would have been the bare earth, dry or wet as the weather might be; and from that couch he would have risen half-poisoned with stench, half-blind with the reek of turf,

and half-mad with the itch.[34]

Or take pre-industrial London, which at the time was one of the wealthiest cities in the world. In the first half of the eighteenth century, child mortality rose as high as 74 percent. Most of the city's population was destitute, living in wretched tenements that would often collapse, killing the occupants. Sanitation was virtually nonexistent, with waste of all sorts being dumped onto the streets. According to one author:

> Overcrowding was severe, and dirt, garbage and filth ubiquitous. A London physician reported that three to eight individuals of differing ages often slept in the same bed, and it was common for those of the lower class to "not put clean sheets on the bed three times a year." . . . Windows, of course, were few; the air, consequently, was not merely bad, but often filled "with putrid excremental effluvia from a vault at the bottom of the staircase." The houses were made of wood, not uncommonly rotting, and "infested with all kinds of vermin." One historian concluded: "From a health point of view the only thing to be said in their favor was that they burned down very easily."[35]

America was a land of riches by comparison. But even in pre-industrial America, most men lived squalid lives compared with what was to come. As late as the mid-1800s, the vast majority of Americans were still yeoman farmers. It's a mistake to romanticize farm life. It was grueling, often hazardous work that left almost no time for leisure—there is a reason why millions fled to the cities when given the opportunity. But pre-industrial cities were only marginally better. "Impoverishment frequently accompanied work in the commercial city," writes historian Thomas Sugrue of the era, "despite the romantic descriptions of early modern life favored by many historians."[36] Work was hard. Conditions were cramped. The streets were filled with waste, pests, and vermin.

Wherever you went—city or countryside—disease was rampant, with malaria and tuberculosis being especially prevalent and feared. As a result, the average lifespan was short—around forty years, with devastatingly high infant mortality rates (although nothing like those in early eighteenth-century London). Those who were lucky enough to make it to early adulthood could expect to live only into their early sixties. "Most people did not survive much past the beginning of today's retirement age," notes historian Jack Larkin.[37]

Not that retirement was an option for most people. Given the low standard of living at the time, you had to work until you died. As Larkin observes:

> Americans bore with many nonfatal but painful and debilitating chronic afflictions. Many men and women did their daily work on limbs that were twisted and painful from dislocations and poorly set fractures. Chronic infections and inflammations of the skin, the stomach, the ears and the genitourinary system could not be treated.[38]

This was the world on the eve of America's Industrial Revolution. The young nation was inching forward; soon, however, it would be taking long, confident strides. The century leading up to the passage of Social Security in 1935 would do more to relieve poverty and increase life's security than any prior century in human history.

- For the first time in history, a people's standard of living increased substantially, generation after generation. U.S. GDP per capita more than quadrupled, growing from $1,287 in 1820 to $5,307 a century later (1990 dollars).[39]
- In just under a century (1850–1930), U.S. life expectancy at birth increased from under forty years to almost sixty.[40]
- Americans were earning more but working less. Between 1870 and 1929, annual work hours plummeted from 3,069 to 2,368.[41]
- All the while, population exploded from 5,308,483 in 1800 to 123,076,741 in 1930.[42]

The numbers do not tell the whole story. The existential circumstances of life were improving by the day. Between 1835 and 1935, medicine advanced (anesthesia, antiseptics, insulin, penicillin, and pasteurization were all developed during this era, along with huge improvements in sanitation), transportation was revolutionized (the internal combustion engine spawned trucks, cars, tractors, and airplanes, while steam trains became far safer thanks to the development of the air brake), new means of communication connected the world (telegraph, telephone, radio), and entrepreneurs filled Americans' homes with electricity, incandescent lighting, sewing machines, washing machines, running water, indoor plumbing, air conditioning, and a whole lot else. People were eating better, dressing better, living better.

By no means were these improvements reserved for the very wealthy. In 1934, in the depths of the Depression, a survey of Pittsburgh found that

> even in the poorest districts in the city, 98 percent of the dwellings had running water (only half had hot water), 91 percent had electricity or gas for lighting, 75 percent had indoor water closets, and 54 percent had a shower or bathtub. This study and others indicate that working-class families of the 1930s had increasing access to utilities and appliances that made housework easier.[43]

What was happening in America? The self-reliant society provided people with an unprecedented degree of *freedom* to produce and *incentive* to produce. Anyone with an idea for how to do things better was free to give it a try. And if he succeeded? The rewards were his to enjoy. The result was an outpouring of ability and ingenuity on a scale the world had never seen.

The Resourcefulness of Free Men

Life, to be sure, was still hard. It had *always* been hard. But it was better than it had ever been and it was improving faster than it ever had, as free individuals lifted themselves out of poverty and into prosperity. Almost everyone saw incremental gains. This itself was unprecedented. But even more astonishing was the fact that a significant and growing proportion of the population was able to rise far beyond its humble beginnings. To take one example, in Boston during the late nineteenth and early twentieth centuries, Stephan Thernstrom concludes that "about a quarter of all the men who first entered the labor market as manual workers ended their careers in a middle-class calling."[44] Other cities saw similar numbers progress.[45]

"We all live in the richest and freest country in the world," said steel titan Andrew Carnegie, "where no man is limited except by his own mental attitude and his own desires."[46] Carnegie was the ultimate testament to that fact. Carnegie had arrived in America as a twelve-year-old Scottish immigrant. With barely a penny to his family's name, and with only five years of formal education behind him, he went to work at a textile mill, twelve hours a day, for $1.20 a week. It wasn't much, but in the land of self-reliance, it was enough.

The job gave Carnegie the opportunity to learn and to demonstrate his dedication to hard work. Very quickly he moved on and up. Less than a year later he had secured a position at O'Reilly's Telegraph Company, starting at more than twice what he had earned at the mill. It was there that Carnegie's rise began in earnest—not through some "lucky break" but through the habit Carnegie would later refer to as "going the extra mile." Carnegie, still working incredibly long days, began going to work early in order to learn how to send and receive telegraph messages. He worked so hard at it that he could eventually take telegraph messages by ear rather than by transcribing the Morse code—a feat only two other people in America could perform. That ability helped him gain the notice of Thomas A. Scott, a superintendent for the Pennsylvania Railroad. And it was through his work with Scott that Carnegie developed the skills and formed the relationships that would enable him to become one of the richest men in history.[47]

Carnegie's degree of success was atypical, but the pattern of his rise was not. It was common, for example, to see ambitious young people start out in business as lowly clerks, learn the ropes of running a business, save money, and eventually strike out on their own. Historian Stuart Blumin describes a typical case:

> When eighteen-year-old William Hoffman began his clerkship in an Albany dry goods store in the spring of 1848 he was given all of the mindless, physically exhausting chores . . . [which included] sweeping the shop, stocking shelves, delivering merchandise to customers, and distributing handbills in the streets. . . . Yet within a month he was being reassured by his employer that perseverance and good work would result in Hoffman's "becoming a Business Man," just as they had for so many who had come before him. As Hoffman and others like him matured and gained experience they were given greater responsibilities—making sales, collecting from customers (including other businessmen) on outstanding accounts, writing letters, even operating the store in the proprietors' absence—and in time many did become proprietors themselves.[48]

The self-reliant did not petulantly demand a "good" job with "good" pay. They seized on any opportunity, no matter the size, and made the most of it.

This was true even for plant and factory workers, including those who sought not to rise to riches but merely to support themselves and their families. They have often been portrayed as laboring in miserable conditions for miserable pay for unendurably long hours at tedious jobs. This was sometimes true. In most cases, though, industrial work was preferable to life on the farm—"Many were driven into the factory system by the deprivations and tedium of farm life," notes one author[49]—and immeasurably better than life before the Industrial Revolution.

In fact, many industrial workers found satisfaction if not joy in their work. "We were proud," recalled Mary Cunion of her days as a weaver in New Hampshire's gigantic Amoskeag manufacturing plant. "I spent my happiest times in the mills. Could you beat that?" The work could sometimes be "drudgery," Cunion admitted, although one is reminded of the economist who observed that while millions spend hours pulling on slot machine levers in Vegas, the most boring job at a factory amounted to pulling a slot machine lever and winning a small prize every time. In any event, even factory work left most workers with a feeling of pride. "I enjoyed every one of my jobs," a co-worker of Cunion said. "We worked a long day but we enjoyed ourselves." Factory workers also tended to earn many times what they could have gotten at "more enjoyable" jobs, which is why many of those who left plants like the Amoskeag soon returned.[50]

But as much as life was improving under capitalism, without a doubt there were new challenges posed by industrialization, notably the prospect of unemployment. But this problem was in fact a huge achievement. For the first time, the vast majority of men were not tied to a single job or a single plot of land. When a self-sufficient farmer had a bad year, he risked starvation. When a factory worker lost his job, he was free to look for another one, which is one reason farmers flocked to the cities. Nevertheless, unemployment was a risk faced by men in an industrial society. What is striking is how well people were able to cope with this challenge—even at that time, when the self-reliant society had only started to enrich them.[51]

Self-reliant Americans knew that sickness, injury, or adverse economic conditions could throw them out of work, and so they prepared for that possibility. "Most families made provisions for the future," notes one researcher. This took a variety of forms. For one thing, they saved, and according to one scholar, "the growth of real incomes in the late nineteenth and early twentieth centuries coincided with a rapid growth of savings. . . . Households tended to save one-eighth to one-ninth of their incomes."[52] For another, they purchased various forms of commercial insurance, especially life and funeral benefits, which not only protected their families in the event of their death, but which could also be converted into cash in case of an emergency. One study found that prior to the Great Depression, "Almost 75 per cent [of the participants] carried insurance—many had several policies—and more than 30 per cent had savings accounts. Only 15 per cent had neither."[53]

Americans in this era also invested in property, be it a house, farm land, or farm animals—"even a garden," note historians Steven Mintz and Susan Kellogg, "provided protection against the financial insecurity caused by temporary unemployment, illness, or old-age." Home ownership "was a particularly valuable source of security, since a family could always obtain an extra income by taking in boarders and lodgers."[54]

Another common strategy was to join one of the many mutual aid societies that existed at the time. These were private associations of individuals that offered an array of affordable member benefits, including various forms of insurance: life, permanent disability, sickness and accident, old-age, and funeral. Between twenty and thirty-five million Americans belonged to mutual aid societies by 1930, more than any other kind of organization besides churches.[55] In the words of one contemporary source, mutual aid societies catered to

> the middle-class workman, the salaried clerk, the farmer, the artisan, the country merchant, and the laborer [seeking to] insure their helpless broods against abject poverty. Rich men insure in the big companies to create an estate; poor men insure in fraternal orders to create bread and meat. It is an insurance against want, the poorhouse, charity, and degradation.[56]

Self-reliant Americans had created their own private safety net. For a small membership fee, they were able to protect themselves against many of life's risks—and millions of them did.

If things did go wrong, then, Americans before the entitlement state generally had options. They could search for odd jobs. They could cut expenses. They could ask non-working family members to find a job. They could turn to insurance and mutual aid. They could draw on their savings and the savings of family members. Indeed, support from family, friends, and neighbors was the most common method of coping with economic challenges, whether through gifts, loans, housing, child care, or some other form of assistance.[57]

If all else failed, an unprecedented amount of private charity was available for those who needed it. "In fact," writes historian Walter Trattner,

> so rapidly did private agencies multiply that before long America's larger cities had what to many people was an embarrassing number of them. Charity directories took as many as 100 pages to list and describe the numerous voluntary agencies that sought to alleviate misery, and combat every imaginable emergency.[58]

In 1910, in New York State, for instance, 151 private benevolent groups provided care for children, and 216 provided care for adults or adults and children.[59] If you were homeless in Chicago in 1933, you could have found shelter at one of the city's 614 YMCAs, or one of the 89 Salvation Army barracks, or one of the seventy-five Goodwill Industries dormitories, among others.[60] During the 1920s, total private philanthropic giving climbed from $21 billion in 1921 to $31.3 billion in 1928 (2009 dollars). To put that in perspective, this was roughly 2.5 percent of GDP. Half a century later, philanthropic spending was about 1.8 percent of GDP.[61]

But charity was almost always a *last* resort. Although it was sometimes necessary, there was widespread recognition that being on the dole was bad for the recipient, economically and spiritually.

The greatest threat to workers was the possibility of widespread, sustained unemployment, but this was rare in capitalist America. From 1900 to 1929, unemployment averaged 4.67 percent, reaching double digits only once (in 1921) and generally staying under 3 percent.[62] Much the same can be said for the period between the Civil War and 1900. Even during the depression of the 1890s, by far the worst period for American workers, unemployment never rose above 8.2 percent, and it stayed under 7 percent for all but four years.[63] (These numbers are all the more impressive when we recall that this was a period of unprecedented immigration, with roughly a million foreigners arriving in America each year, most of them poor, uneducated, and unskilled.[64])

How did Americans in the era before entitlements fare in old age? One indication is that, as late as World War I, even those pushing for an American entitlement state did not argue that old age was a major source of poverty and insecurity in the United States.[65] In Massachusetts, for example, fewer than 8 percent of residents sixty-five or older were dependent, in part or in whole, on charity or government welfare in 1910. For all but six states, the number of elderly paupers—citizens chronically dependent on charity or welfare—was less than two thousand in 1923, and in twelve states there were fewer than 150. In London, the richest city in the world at the time, 14.8 percent of residents sixty or older were counted as paupers. In both cases, of course, this represented an advance from earlier eras, where few people ever saw age sixty.[66]

Typically, elderly Americans continued to support themselves through productive work until the end of their lives. This was seldom a tragic necessity. Most did not *want* to retire. They took pride and found meaning in their work. The prospect of spending their final years sitting at home without purpose or aim was hardly enticing. "[I]t was not until the period after World War II," writes sociologist John Myles, "that the retirement principle was successfully 'sold' to the U.S. working class."[67]

One popular myth claims that industrialization threw the elderly out of work in hordes. Although the elderly as a group did have higher unemployment rates than the rest of the adult population, that had been equally true prior to industrialization. In Massachusetts, for instance, the economy moved from primarily agrarian in 1840 to primarily industrial in 1885, and yet employment among men over sixty remained at roughly 70 percent over that time span.[68]

For those who did want to (or have to) stop working, there were three main methods for financing retirement prior to the entitlement state: savings, private pensions, and family support. With low government spending, there was virtually no price inflation during this era, so savers were rewarded: What they stocked away during their working years retained virtually all of its purchasing power when it came time to retire. Private pensions were growing in popularity as well. "Most industries or firms adopted the railroad pension formula," notes historian Roy Lubove. "The beneficiary received 1 percent of his average monthly pay for ten years preceding retirement, multiplied by the number of years of service."[69] Meanwhile, the vast majority of non-working elderly lived with children or other family members. Thanks to these methods, more and more people who wanted to retire from work were able to do so.

Sadly, there were cases in which older Americans could not continue working and lacked the means to support themselves. Some of these people were helped by private charity. By the 1930s, for instance, there were roughly twelve hundred privately funded benevolent homes for the elderly.[70] In other cases, though, private efforts were supplanted by government poorhouses, where conditions ranged from tolerable to wretched. Although only 2 percent of the elderly were ever subjected to such institutions (a number that was declining in the decades before the New Deal), opponents of the self-reliant society would stoke fear of the poorhouse to launch their push for Social Security.[71]

In sum, there were challenges associated with industrialization, but they were not unmanageable, and Americans were committed to solving them through private, voluntary action. They did not believe that the way to solve problems was by restricting freedom, and they found that the challenges they did face were diminishing as the economy progressed. Above all, those challenges paled in comparison to the staggering benefits individuals, including the elderly, were reaping from industrial capitalism.

Cracks in the Foundation

American society has never been a monolith. From the start, there were elements that clashed with the ethic of self-reliance. At the same time that self-reliance was esteemed, so was the notion that "I am my brother's keeper."

"Put yourself in the place of every poor man and deal with him as you would God deal with you," John Wesley had said in the eighteenth century.[72] Religious leaders reminded their parishioners of the Bible's mandate to "not be hardhearted or tightfisted toward your poor brother [but] be openhanded and freely lend him whatever he needs."[73] If America was unique in extolling the individual's pursuit of happiness, it inherited from Europe the doctrine that the individual's duty is to serve the poor and the meek. The American soul was a mixture—a mixture of self-reliance and selfless service to others.

From the founding era through the early twentieth century, the "brother's keeper" view was generally taken to mean that each individual had a sacred obligation to support his own life *if he could*—but if he could not, it was the responsibility of society to take care of him. Although to be one of the kept was not an enviable position, the deserving poor *deserved*—they were owed help. And even the undeserving poor ought to receive some minimal assistance, most believed. In short, helping those in need was morally obligatory.

"For the most part," writes one historian, "the redistribution of wealth was to be made voluntarily, encouraged by religious admonitions, or by the pressure of consumer strikes, and union demands."[74] America's abundant system of private charity was thus a result of mixed motives: the benevolence of self-reliant individuals, and a belief that serving those in need was a moral duty. That duty was to be shouldered primarily by individuals. But there were, in fact, government handout programs from the start, coming mainly in the form of "outdoor relief" (more or less the equivalent of a modern welfare program, although benefits would often consist of food rather than cash) or poorhouses. By today's standards, however, these efforts were miniscule, although they were growing in the years leading up to Social Security. "For example," writes Cato Institute scholar Michael Tanner, "between 1911 and 1925, the amount of outdoor relief dispensed in the nation's 16 largest cities increased from $1.6 million to $14.7 million."[75] Other welfare programs, most aimed at helping widows and orphans, also existed during this era. (Aside from veterans' benefits, efforts aimed specifically at the elderly were scant; as a group, their conditions were regarded as "comparatively good."[76])

Americans generally didn't see a conflict between these relatively small state efforts to relieve people's economic troubles and a limited, rights-protecting government—just as they didn't see a conflict between Christian service and ambitious self-reliance. In the decades ahead the conflict would become apparent.

The American way of life—limited government, capitalism, and the self-reliant society—produced the freest, most prosperous, most moral society in history. It would not last. During the twentieth century, opponents of the American system would exploit the rift between American self-reliance and the belief in self-sacrifice. They would point out that if we are our brother's keeper, then our brother has a right to be kept—and it is the state's duty to enforce that right. Their beachhead would be the Social Security Act of 1935.

CHAPTER TWO

Establishing Social Security (1880–1935)

It is often said that the Great Depression led to the creation of Social Security in 1935. This is only partly true. The full truth is that a group of ideologues—history has labeled them "Progressives" and "liberals," but a better name for them is "entitlement statists" for reasons that will become clear—used the Depression to establish Social Security and move toward their long-held goal of transforming America from a self-reliant society to an entitlement society. For the first time, significant numbers of Americans would look to the state to support their lives. For the first time, the state would redistribute vast sums of their wealth. For the first time, men's most personal economic decisions would be overseen and directed by politicians and bureaucrats. Self-reliance would no longer be the keystone of the system.

But that is not how the supporters of Social Security described their project publicly. While statist academics, journalists, and other intellectuals would openly attack the self-reliant society, their fellow travelers in Washington were more cautious. Franklin D. Roosevelt and the New Dealers would claim that theirs was a pragmatic effort to overcome challenges made apparent by the Depression. Industrialization made life insecure, and this could only be overcome through entitlement programs, such as government-provided unemployment insurance and old-age retirement benefits. These entitlements would not alter the character of America or its system of government, they said. They were not revolutions but reforms—reforms consistent with America's traditions of limited government and individual responsibility. In the words of historian W. Andrew Achenbaum:

> [T]he president emphasized that such intervention merely reinforced long-standing American commitments to self-reliance and mutual responsibility. FDR acted because of the immediate crisis and his commitment to Progressive principles. But he did not intend to displace American self-reliance and capitalist principles with a federal Leviathan.[77]

According to Roosevelt, Social Security was not a revolution in American values, but a quintessentially American program and nothing less could provide Americans with the security they rightfully deserved. "Our task of reconstruction does not require the creation of new and strange values," Roosevelt protested.

> It is rather the finding of the way once more to known, but to some degree forgotten, ideas and values. If the means and details are in some instances new, the objectives are as permanent as human nature.[78]

He doth protest too much. Roosevelt felt a desperate need to assure Americans that he was not altering American values because he very obviously was. To pass Social Security, he had to.

Old-age entitlements were not a new idea—entitlement statists had been advocating them for half a century. But the American public resisted, regarding the scheme as an affront to property rights, limited government, and the ethic of self-reliance. To foist the beginnings of an entitlement state on a people who did not believe in entitlement was an audacious goal, requiring entitlement statists to rewrite the story of America and recast the story of entitlements.

The Un-American Origins of Social Security

To understand the true nature of what the New Dealers sought to achieve, we need to look back at the origins of the entitlement state and of the campaign to impose entitlements on America. Social Security was the brainchild of a group of intellectuals who had tried for decades to transform America from a self-reliant society into an entitlement state. The earliest entitlement statists—men and women such as Louis Brandeis, Woodrow Wilson, Jane Addams, and Herbert Croly—labeled themselves "Progressives."

"The welfare-state policies of the twentieth and now twenty-first century are built upon a direct and conscious rejection of the original principles of the American Constitution," write Ronald Pestritto and William Atto in their edited collection *American Progressivism: A Reader*. Progressivism, they explain, is

> an argument to progress, or to move beyond, the political principles of the American founding. It is an argument to

enlarge vastly the scope of national government for the purpose of responding to a set of economic and social conditions which, progressives contend, could not have been envisioned at the founding and for which the founders' limited, constitutional government was inadequate.[79]

The Progressives were open about their opposition to the founding principles of America. The Founders had said that the purpose of government was to protect men's inalienable individual rights. Herbert Croly balked at this notion, urging that "every popular government should in the end . . . possess the power of taking any action, which, in the opinion of a decisive majority of the people, is demanded by the public welfare." As if that weren't clear enough, he went on: "The time may come when the fulfillment of a justifiable democratic purpose may demand the limitation of certain rights, to which the Constitution affords such guarantees."[80]

Take the Progressive attitude toward private property rights. In a passage that sums up the early American mind, the eminent English jurist William Blackstone wrote, "So great moreover is the regard of the law for private property that it will not authorize the least violation of it; no, not even for the general good of the whole community."[81] The Progressives disagreed. "[E]very man holds his property subject to the general right of the community to regulate its use to whatever degree the public welfare may require it," said America's first Progressive president, Theodore Roosevelt, in 1910.[82]

Our next Progressive president was even more open in his contempt for America's founding principles. "You know that it was Jefferson," recalled Woodrow Wilson, "who said that the best government is that which does as little governing as possible. . . . But that time is passed."[83] Instead of a limited government, he wrote elsewhere, "Government does now whatever experience permits or the times demand."[84] To limit government, in the Progressives' view, was like tying a parent's hands and making him stand by helplessly as his children run into traffic. The government, they believed, did not need limits but *power*: It had to be powerful enough to do whatever Progressives thought "the national interest" required.

This was an ideology deeply hostile toward individualism and capitalism, and suspicious of America's entire self-reliant society. The Progressives, borrowing heavily from European socialists, wanted Americans to forswear their own happiness and devote themselves, in Croly's words, to "individual subordination and self-denial" for the sake of the collective. ("[T]his necessity of subordinating the satisfaction of individual desires to the fulfillment of a national purpose," he added, "is attached particularly to the absorbing occupation of the American people, —the occupation, viz.: of accumulating wealth.") Whereas most Americans were torn between a belief in self-reliance and self-sacrifice, the Progressives, like the socialists, were remarkably consistent. It was morally *wrong*, they said, to place any consideration above your duty to be your brother's—or your grandfather's—keeper.[85]

The Progressives, to be sure, were not by and large socialists, but they were driven by the core of the socialist ideology—the doctrine that, in Ayn Rand's words,

> man has no right to exist for his own sake, that his life and his work do not belong to *him*, but belong to society, that the only justification of his existence is his service to society, and that society may dispose of him in any way it pleases for the sake of whatever it deems to be its own tribal, collective good.[86]

The Progressives shared the socialists' goals, but argued that the way to bring them about was through partial, not total, control of the economy. Socialism claimed to improve men's economic well-being by putting the government in control of the *production* of wealth; Progressivism emphasized government control of the *distribution* of wealth. Thus a central pillar of the Progressive program became the creation of an American entitlement state, which would ensure that wealth found its way from those who earned it to those who allegedly needed it.

The push for an American entitlement state began with the "social insurance" movement, spearheaded by Progressives Richard T. Ely and John R. Commons. (A recent book on Social Security calls Commons "Social Security's grandfather."[87]) Unlike traditional forms of means-tested welfare, which subsidize people with low incomes, social insurance would not be means-tested. It was meant for those who could generally support themselves, and was intended to provide them with protection from burdensome and typically unforeseen costs: unemployment, disease, injury, the inability to work due to old age, and the like. It was said to be insurance *against* becoming unable to support oneself.

Whereas traditional welfare programs rewarded people for being "needy," social insurance programs would reward people to prevent them from becoming needy. In both cases, however, the goal was the same: for society to support "the needy." What made these programs "social"? People, it was claimed, could not or would not voluntarily join such programs, so they had to be compelled by government to participate. They would pay taxes to finance the system, and this in turn would make them eligible for benefits.

Social insurance thus blended together two issues: the need to deal with the challenges an individual faced in an industrial economy, and the desire on the part of entitlement statists to redistribute wealth to "the needy." In the words of leading Social Security expert Carolyn Weaver:

> [S]ocial insurance had two functions: compensating workers for interruptions in earnings and raising their standard of living. While the insurance function could certainly have been met through alternative (private and voluntary) means, the redistributive function required coercive state action.[88]

According to the entitlement statists, if Americans wanted to protect themselves against risks such as old age and unemployment, they had no choice but to embrace wealth redistribution.

Social insurance had its origins in Germany. During the 1880s, German chancellor Otto von Bismarck pushed a series of social insurance measures, including an old-age pension program. In part, Bismarck was trying to take the wind out of the sails of radical German socialist groups by embracing some of the more popular policies they advocated, admitting that "It may be State Socialism, but it is necessary."[89] But the entitlement state was not merely some cynical ploy for power. Bismarck also believed in its nobility. Laying out his moral justification of entitlements, Bismarck called it

> the modern state idea, the result of Christian ethics, according to which the state should discharge, besides the defensive duty of protecting existing rights, the positive duty of promoting the welfare of all its members, and especially those who are weak and in need of help, by means of judicious institutions and the employment of those resources for the community which are at its disposal.[90]

The world was watching, and although much of Europe would soon follow in Germany's footsteps, America would not. America's ambassador to Germany, Andrew White, would write to the State

Department in 1881, arguing that

> the idea that underlies and permeates . . . all [Germany's entitlement policies] is socialistic—the idea that the advancement of the laboring classes is to be left not merely or mainly to individual foresight or energy but to society as a whole, acting through its constituted authorities.

The German model, he concluded wryly, is "based on the theory that 'that government is best which governs *most*.'"[91] The American people, by and large, agreed with White's assessment. They had no interest in socialist ideas. But the American Progressives did.

Ely, who had studied in Germany during the late 1870s, and Commons, who had studied under Ely, would form the most influential Progressive social insurance organization, the American Association for Labor Legislation. The AALL's membership roster reads like a Who's Who of Progressive luminaries, including Louis Brandeis, Woodrow Wilson, and Jane Addams, as well as the lesser known Isaac Rubinow, whose 1913 book *Social Insurance* would heavily influence FDR's thinking about government old-age handouts. "Rubinow's views and those of certain of his outspoken colleagues," noted Weaver,

> attacked the core of what had come to be known as traditional American values: thrift, self-reliance, and the market-system as a means of organizing society. Their views revealed most starkly the development of a new prevention-insurance rhetoric for what were inherently redistribution programs.[92]

These Progressives would fight, mostly at the state and local level, for various social insurance schemes throughout the early part of the twentieth century.

But these early social insurance efforts met with limited success. As one scholar notes, the advocates "faced strong ideological and institutional obstacles that hindered their attempts to push for the enactment of" entitlement measures.[93] There was simply too much admiration and respect for the country's founding principles and "traditional American values" for them to make significant headway.

That would change with Franklin Delano Roosevelt's arrival on the political scene. Roosevelt would keep the essence of Progressivism, but would alter its rhetoric. He would reframe Progressivism, not as a rejection of American ideals, but as their realization. He would help undo the self-reliant society, all the while claiming that he was its savior.

Selling Social Security

FDR openly acknowledged his debt to Progressive leaders, such as Woodrow Wilson and Theodore Roosevelt. But whereas they had failed to enact entitlements in America, he would succeed. How did he do it?

Above all, Roosevelt was the beneficiary of the march of time. Although Americans resisted statism—the notion that the individual's life and wealth belong to the state—statist ideas gradually came to permeate the culture in the decades leading up to Social Security. At church, the exhortation to be your brother's keeper was continually hammered into people's minds. The schools, meanwhile, became dominated by academics increasingly hostile to the American system and the Enlightenment principles on which it was based. By the 1930s, most Americans had been educated by professors who rejected reason, individualism, capitalism, and self-reliance.[94]

These statist intellectuals were chipping away at Americans' reverence for self-reliance. When they were not openly challenging it, they were hard at work demoting it in moral stature. Sure, they said, self-reliance is a fine thing to aspire to, but it is no great virtue. It amounts to "mere prudence" and can easily collapse into abject greed and mean-spiritedness. What's more, they argued, those who were not self-reliant did not deserve moral blame or even pity, but compassion and sympathy. They were, by and large, victims of their parents, their genes, their class, or American society as a whole. The intellectuals severed the link between irresponsibility and dependence, declaring in the words of one social worker that the "belief that under ordinary conditions people are in need through some fault of their own" was "outmoded."[95] Abject failure, they said, could happen to anyone, at any time. Those who were lucky enough to succeed should not ascribe it to their own virtue, but to dumb luck. The American motto, according to the Progressive vision, should not be "Make something of yourself" but "There but for the grace of God go I."[96]

Whatever resistance the Progressives encountered, they met with no *intellectual* opposition. Even so, by the late 1920s, Americans were still not fully ready to embrace the entitlement state. They were, however, willing to make room for it at the margins, and, more important perhaps, they no longer seemed fully comfortable opposing it. Entitlements did not, during the Roaring Twenties, seem necessary—but neither were they disreputable. Entitlement statists even succeeded in establishing government pension programs in a few of the more Progressive states during this period.

By the time the Great Depression hit, the pieces were in place. All the entitlement statists needed was someone able to overcome the last vestiges of entitlement skepticism. Enter FDR and the New Dealers. They blasted through the American people's lingering suspicion of statist policies with a campaign to help rewrite history and the nation's political lexicon.

"The civilization of the past hundred years," Franklin D. Roosevelt said upon signing the Social Security Act of 1935, "with its startling industrial changes, has tended more and more to make life insecure."[97] This was a ludicrous claim. Industrial capitalism had made life more secure than it had ever been. But pre-capitalism's legacy of poverty could not be erased overnight, and this allowed entitlement statists to point to the remaining pockets of poverty, blame them on capitalism, and offer the entitlement state as the only solution. Indeed, the entitlement statists did more than that. As historian Thomas J. Sugrue notes, they went into the "bleakest sections" of cities and crafted "sensational descriptions of the small, highly visible districts of vice," dishonestly holding them up "as representative of American cities." (Today, he adds, their accounts continue to be "accepted uncritically by many twentieth-century scholars.")[98]

In addition to dismissing and downplaying the rise in prosperity made possible by capitalism, the entitlement statists went on to make two further claims.

First, they claimed that the old ways of coping with industrialization's challenges could no longer work. Roosevelt, for instance, acknowledged that people had historically been able to turn to their families and communities for support in tough times, but claimed that "The complexities of great communities and of organized industry make less real these simple means of security."[99] It was, at best, a gross exaggeration. Family ties had generally remained strong during America's transition from the farms to the cities, and social bonds in urban neighborhoods were not markedly weaker than in rural communities.[100] Remarking on life in the cities in the era between the Civil War and World War I, historian Walter Trattner (himself a supporter of the entitlement state) notes that "the vast majority" of those in need were able to rely on

> family, kin, and neighbors for aid, including the landlord, who sometimes deferred rent; the local butcher or grocer, who frequently carried them for a while by allowing bills to go unpaid; and the local saloonkeeper, who often came to their aid by providing loans and outright gifts, including free meals, and on occasion, temporary jobs.[101]

Second, the entitlement statists claimed that their programs were not new in substance, but were mere extensions of existing private, voluntary efforts for helping those in need: mutual aid societies and private charities. If Americans would only stop making such a sharp distinction between private, voluntary efforts and coercive government schemes, the New Dealers held, they would see that the entitlement state was perfectly compatible with American ideals.

Undoubtedly, the most significant case of historical revisionism had to do with the Great Depression. Before the Depression, Americans felt largely in control of their own economic destiny. Economic freedom provided them with the security of knowing that no one could interfere with their pursuit of prosperity. As a consequence, accepting handouts was regarded as shameful, except in those rare circumstances where a person, through no fault of his own, truly could not support himself. But what if they weren't in control of their destiny? What if, thanks to forces built into the capitalist system, anyone, at any time could end up out of work for months or even years? What if that could happen on so large a scale that private charity would be unable to cope with it? Then perhaps the dole was not so shameful. Maybe we *needed* government to step in to protect us.

That was precisely the story Americans were told in the wake of the Great Depression. The Depression was the product of uncontrolled capitalism, said the entitlement statists, and only government intervention could get America through it and out of it. Long term, they added, it was vital to develop entitlement programs, such as Social Security, in order to prevent millions from falling into need in the first place.

Some of the leading economists of the age pointed out that capitalism had hardly been "uncontrolled" in the years leading up to the Great Depression. Eminent scholars such as Ludwig von Mises and F. A. Hayek observed that government had been exercising immense power over the economy, particularly in the areas of money and banking that took center stage in the collapse. They argued that Hoover and Roosevelt, instead of cutting government intervention after the crash, intervened in the economy on a scale never rivaled during peacetime. The government pressured business to keep wages high, stoking unemployment. The protectionist Smoot-Hawley Tariff crippled foreign trade. Early New Deal efforts such as the National Recovery Act scared off new investment in the economy. Meanwhile, the Federal Reserve in its conduct of monetary policy loosened credit when they should have tightened it and tightened it when they should have loosened it. Absent those or similar factors, they said, there was no reason that the economy should collapse into depression. But these economists were largely ignored as a new breed of statist economists rose to prominence—most notably John Maynard Keynes, who brought government the good news: The solution to all of their troubles was to spend more of the public's money.[102]

At the same time that the Depression was being blamed on capitalism, its effects were being deliberately exaggerated by those who desired to introduce the entitlement state to America's shores. As historian Clarence Carson points out, "most peoples of the world if placed in the United States in the 1930s would have been struck rather by the prosperity than the poverty." What made the Depression so remarkable was the contrast between the riches (and security) industrial capitalism had created, and the prospect of stagnation and mass unemployment. But for the non-capitalist world, America remained a land of riches. According to Carson:

> When the movie *The Grapes of Wrath*, which depicted the story of a migrant family from Oklahoma in its move to California, was shown in [Communist] Russia, many were impressed not with the deprivation of the Joad family but by the fact that they owned a car.[103]

The point isn't just that Depression-era America was better than any-era Communist Russia. As Carson observes, most people were working and went on with life, "though there were some alterations in the rhythms and the pace." He gives a litany of examples, from a best-seller list which was strikingly apolitical and non-economic in concern to improved cars, to the rise of Big Band swing, to a golden age of movies, including *Gone With the Wind*. This was not a decade filled with masses of starving Americans and justifying a radical departure from the principles of the Founders. It was a rocky decade, very painful for some, anxiety-tinged for many, but manageable for most.[104]

Whatever the case, the Great Depression was viewed as a crisis of capitalism, and this opened the door to radical change. Even so, Americans would probably not have embraced the entitlement state were it not for FDR's new rhetorical strategy. Instead of openly admitting that he wanted to transform America's free enterprise system, as the Progressives had, FDR would claim that he merely wanted to make it more secure. As scholar William Voegeli explains:

> FDR, beginning in his campaign for the presidency in 1932, insistently framed the question of expanding government in terms of upholding and updating the founding . . . rather than repudiating it. According to Sidney Milkis, "FDR's deft reinterpretation of the American constitutional tradition" gave "legitimacy to progressive principles by embedding them in the language of constitutionalism and interpreting them as an expansion rather than a subversion of the natural rights tradition." Significantly, FDR conveyed this orientation by enthusiastically embracing "liberalism" as the designation for the New Deal's philosophy, sending the term "progressivism," with its clearly implied critique of the American founding, into long exile. To do so he wrested "liberalism" away from the defenders of limited government, who acceded unhappily to calling themselves "conservatives."[105]

To hear FDR and the New Dealers tell it, they weren't against the Constitution—the Constitution was a "living document" that needed to change with changing circumstances. They weren't against individual rights—they were *expanding* the existing set of rights: not just a right to life, liberty, property, and the pursuit of happiness, but a right to a job, food, clothing, shelter, medical care, education, and recreation, among others. They weren't against freedom, which traditionally meant freedom from the coercive might of other human beings—they simply aimed to free us from want and fear as well.

But wasn't the Constitution designed as a limited grant of power to the federal government in order to achieve the ends laid out in the Declaration of Independence: securing the individual rights of man? Didn't those rights protect the individual's freedom and property from coercion by others? And didn't these new "rights" and "freedoms" *necessitate* coercing others? Since nature didn't provide people with jobs, food, medical care, or a retirement, wasn't the only way to grant those "rights"—to violate the rights of the people forced to provide or pay for them? Could you really have a *right* to violate others' rights? No one stepped forward to raise those questions at the time, and the New Dealers certainly were happy to avoid them.

The Repeal of the Self-Reliant Society

All of these threads—the decades-long crusade for entitlements, worries caused by the Depression, the New Dealers' bag of rhetorical tricks—came together to produce the Social Security Act of 1935.

Revealingly, it was not the public who asked for Social Security—it was the entitlement statists who introduced and crusaded for Social Security in the face of public skepticism. Even in the midst of the Depression, Americans "feared the creation of a welfare state," notes historian W. Andrew Achenbaum.[106] The New Dealers were able to allay these fears by assuring Americans that Social Security was a way to help others *and* help yourself. With Social Security, they said, you could do the moral thing—ensure that the needy elderly were taken care of—and you would benefit in the process, since you would one day receive benefits. You could be your brother's keeper—by supporting a system that would also help *you* remain self-reliant in old age, since your eventual Social Security check would not be a handout but an "earned benefit" you had paid for during your working years.

How did Social Security's opponents respond to all of this? Rather than defend America's robust private safety net and attack Social Security for creating an un-American entitlement state—the thing Americans most feared about the proposal—opponents by and large *endorsed* the goal of creating an entitlement state, and bickered with FDR and the New Dealers only over the details of the Act.

Kansas governor Alf Landon, who would challenge FDR for the presidency in 1936, hailed New Dealers as acting from "a warm heart and a generous impulse." Assuring his audience that he was all for "social justice" and conceding that "it is a responsibility of society to take care . . . [of those] unable to provide for their old age," Landon nevertheless resisted Social Security. The New Dealers might very well be pursuing the proper moral goal, Landon admitted, but their means were misguided: "It is a glaring example of the bungling and waste that have characterized this administration's attempts to fulfill its benevolent purposes." In his strongest statement, he denounced the Social Security Act as "unjust, unworkable, stupidly drafted and wastefully financed." Nevertheless, he concluded, its failing was not that it transformed the United States into an entitlement state, but that "It endangers the whole cause of social security in this country." His proposed solution? To "provide for every American citizen over 65 the supplementary payment necessary to give a minimum income sufficient to protect him or her from want." The conservative answer to "social insurance" was undisguised welfare. The left promised a guaranteed "earned income" to everyone who paid in to the system—the right promised handouts to "the needy."[107]

Americans were never offered a political choice between capitalism and statism, between self-reliance and entitlement. They were offered only a choice between two forms of the entitlement state, and any reservations they may have had were met with the assurance that the philosophy of individual responsibility was compatible with the collectivist ideal of "social responsibility." The Republicans did not defend the self-reliant society and expose Social Security as a threat to that society. They fell over themselves to praise "social responsibility," "social justice," and the nobility of the entitlement statists' goals. Whatever resistance there was among the public to FDR's remaking of America did not find a voice among the country's political or intellectual leadership.

The entitlement statists won. And despite their rhetorical nod to self-reliance, "earned benefits," and "saving capitalism," the meaning of their victory was clear. According to Trattner:

> For the first time in American history, funds to finance all or part of the needs of selected groups in the population become a permanent item in the federal budget, one that has continued to grow each year. With the S.S.A. (and other New Deal programs), which introduced the idea of *entitlement* into national policy, the federal government assumed responsibility for the welfare of most, if not all, of its citizens; hence, the American welfare state was born.[108]

Social Security inaugurated the American entitlement state. It ushered in a social system in which individual rights, property rights, limited government, voluntary cooperation, and self-reliance were all dispensable. The entitlement state was thus a radical departure from the Founding Fathers' creation.

The Social Security Act should be seen as the repeal of the self-reliant society. By 1935, America was on its way to becoming a land of intrusive government and dependence.

It was just the beginning.

CHAPTER THREE

Completing the System (1935–1939)

The Social Security Act of 1935 covered far more than old-age pensions. Title I was a means-tested welfare program for the elderly, designed primarily as a short-term method for helping victims of the Depression. Titles III and IX dealt with support for the unemployed. Title IV, which would eventually grow into the program we typically think of as "welfare," provided $25 million in aid to families with dependent children. Title X provided $3 million to the blind. But none of these programs would approach the size and scale of Title II's retirement scheme.[109]

Inside Washington, there had been general agreement that some sort of retirement handout should be passed, but there was violent disagreement over its details. Above all, the question was how to finance this unprecedented program.

From the start, FDR insisted that Social Security's retirement handouts should be financed through a separate payroll tax, not through the government's general tax revenues. Each person's handouts would then be scaled against his contribution to the program; the more he paid in payroll taxes, the greater his handouts. This was critical if Americans were to view Social Security, not as an unearned entitlement, but as an "earned benefit." As Roosevelt would later admit to one of his advisors:

> We put those pay roll contributions there so as to give the contributors a legal, moral, and political right to collect their pensions and their unemployment benefits. With those taxes in there, no damn politician can ever scrap my social security program. Those taxes aren't a matter of economics, they're straight politics.[110]

This was how FDR intended to reconcile Social Security with self-reliance. Social Security was to be presented to the public as little more than a commercial retirement plan run not by a private insurance company but by the government. You paid into the account through special taxes during your working years, and eventually you would receive back your savings plus interest, enabling you to remain a self-supporting citizen during your golden years. If Social Security payments came out of the government's general revenues, the president recognized, this narrative would be far less plausible.

FDR got his way. The 1935 act was funded by a 2 percent tax on wages up to a $3,000 cap, with half of those taxes ostensibly paid by the employer. That percentage was scheduled to grow by increments from 2 percent to 6 percent twelve years later. A pamphlet the government created to promote Social Security assured the public, "That is the most you will ever pay."[111]

It was a particularly egregious lie in a campaign built on lies. It was understood by Social Security's architects that the payroll tax would have to grow beyond 6 percent once the program matured. It was also understood by economists that the division between the employee's and the employer's half of the payroll tax was artificial, and that the full tax would effectively come out of the employee's pay in the form of lower wages. But the entitlement statists wanted to conceal the true costs of the program in order to overcome public skepticism. They maintained that their "noble" ends justified their sordid means.

Covering up the true costs of the program was part of a larger pattern of behavior in which the originators of Social Security were willing to do almost anything to get some sort of entitlement program established, believing—correctly, it would turn out—that it would be easier to grow the program once it was in place than to get everything they wanted at the start. Thus, for example, the original program was not universal. It excluded more than nine million workers, including farmers, domestic servants, and government employees. Additionally, it would not cover those who had not worked for at least five years in a covered occupation by the time they retired. These were pragmatic concessions from the program's architects, who desired a universal system but believed it to be unfeasible at the time. As FDR would say, "The place of such a fundamental in our future civilization is too precious to be jeopardized now by extravagant action."[112] This was a clear admission that the entitlement statists had a grand vision for America—but by no means were they going to share that full vision with the people, lest they find themselves rebuffed.

Although the New Dealers did not want Social Security to be perceived as a handout, their goal was in fact to guarantee people income on the basis of their need rather than productive achievement. As a result, they were eager to pay people benefits out of proportion to their tax "contributions" whenever they thought they could get away with it. In the end, the original 1935 act would feature subsidies for low-income participants, who would receive greater handouts relative to their earnings than would high-income participants, as well as for the first wave of retirees, who would receive a lifetime of handouts after paying Social Security taxes for only a few years. The first Social Security recipient paid a total of $24.75 in payroll taxes—and ended up collecting $22,888.92 in lifetime handouts.[113]

In sum, the 1935 act established the core of Social Security as we know it today. It would be funded through special payroll taxes, and handouts would be linked to individual contributions, with some amount of redistribution baked into the formula. But unlike the mature program, it would cover only a segment of workers, and both its level of taxes and handouts would be relatively low.

The Constitutional Question

The major question the New Dealers faced after the passage of Social Security was whether it would hold up constitutionally. There were reasons to doubt it. Earlier New Deal interventions had been rebuffed by the Supreme Court, and another pension law—the Railroad Retirement Act—had been found unconstitutional just that year on the grounds that it violated the Fifth Amendment's due process clause by "taking the property of one and giving it to another."[114]

The New Dealers knew that their program, taken as a whole, was not authorized by the Constitution. Nowhere did the founding document give Congress the power to start a massive pension entitlement. The New Dealers' hope was that the Court would find the payroll taxes constitutional on the basis of Congress's taxing power, and the handouts constitutional under their spending power. This led lawmakers to artificially separate the pension plan from its financing provisions, going so far as to describe them under separate titles of the Social Security Act.

In addition, although the New Dealers had pitched Social Security to the public as an insurance program rather than an entitlement, they performed an about-face for the Supreme Court. Since the Constitution did not authorize a government-run insurance program, they made sure to strip any insurance language from the bill.

They needn't have worried. To their surprise, the Court gave Social Security its blessing based on the Constitution's "general welfare" provision. It was a dubious decision, to say the least. As James Madison had pointed out more than a century earlier, the "general welfare" clause did not add to Congress's enumerated powers. To take the term "general welfare," wrote Madison, "in a literal and unlimited sense would be a metamorphosis of the Constitution into a character which there is a host of proofs was not contemplated by its creators."[115] Nevertheless, that was how the Court found. According to Social Security historians Sylvester Schieber and John Shoven:

> This meant that the careful separation between the tax and the benefit provisions of the act was unnecessary. It meant that the legislation could be based on the principles of social insurance, but also that the language of the legislation could be construed according to that of social insurance.[116]

The New Dealers would soon cash in on this opportunity. As part of their effort to reconcile Social Security with the self-reliant society, they enveloped the entitlement program in the reassuring language of insurance. They changed the name of the Bureau of Old-Age Benefits to the Bureau of Old-Age Insurance and replaced terms like "taxes" with insurance-laden terminology, such as "premiums" and "contributions." FICA, what we call the payroll taxes that fund Social Security, stands for "the Federal Insurance Contributions Act."[117] The idea was that if Social Security was seen as insurance rather than welfare, recipients would feel that they were remaining self-reliant: They were supporting themselves in old age, not accepting charity or taking handouts from the government.

But the "insurance" rhetoric was merely one more lie intended to dupe Americans into believing they were getting an earned benefit rather than an unearned entitlement. Arthur J. Altmeyer, for instance, one of the leading architects of Social Security, would later testify that "There is no individual contract between the beneficiary and the government . . . there are no vested rights." A 1960 Supreme Court decision, *Flemming v. Nestor*, would explicitly deny the insurance and earned-right conceptions of the program. As Justice John Harlan wrote, "To engraft upon the Social Security System a concept of 'accrued property rights' would deprive it of the flexibility and boldness in adjustment to the ever-changing conditions it demands." (In his dissent, Justice Hugo Black replied that "People who pay premiums for insurance usually think they are paying for insurance, not for 'flexibility and boldness.'")[118] Economist and legal scholar Charlotte Twight sums up the matter this way:

> The insurance analogy enabled government officials to falsely characterize Social Security benefits as a contractual right, an earned benefit. . . . It is one of the most flagrant deceptions at the heart of Social Security. While Social Security officials have avowed publicly that "old age insurance" entails "retirement annuities payable as a matter of right," both program officials and courts have stated elsewhere that recipients do *not* have contractual rights to their benefits, but instead are dependent on congressional good will for any benefits they may receive during their retirement.[119]

The 1939 Amendments

In 1939, the architects of Social Security settled a debate about how to fund the program. Although Americans would be encouraged to think of Social Security as a gigantic savings program, there would be no savings. Social Security would in fact be a "pay-as-you-go" system. This was a ridiculous euphemism for turning Social Security into an intergenerational wealth transfer scheme, in which current workers would be taxed to pay for handouts to current retirees. Those workers would receive nothing in return except the hope that they would be able to do the same thing to younger Americans once they retired.

The great advantage of this setup, its advocates said, is that each generation would be able to receive far more in handouts than it ever paid in taxes, since the younger generation could always be expected to grow in population and in taxable income. Some worried that this made Social Security into a Ponzi scheme.[120] The architects of the program were unmoved. Economist Paul Samuelson would later go so far as to *praise* the pay-go approach as "the greatest Ponzi game ever contrived." Its beauty, he would say, was precisely "that it is actuarially unsound. Everyone who reaches retirement age is given benefit privileges that far exceed anything he has paid in."[121] A true Ponzi scheme had to collapse, but so long as there is a growing workforce and a growing economy to support retirees, Social Security faced no such problem, Samuelson argued. And as far as pay-go supporters were concerned, those conditions were expected to hold "as far ahead as the eye cannot see."[122]

But what if those conditions did not hold? What if, say, a baby boom generation produced far fewer offspring than its parents' generation or the economy failed to perform as well as expected? Either taxes would shoot up or handouts would have to be slashed or the system itself might become unsustainable. In that case, calling Social Security a "Ponzi scheme" may not be far from the truth.

Such concerns seemed remote during the 1930s, however, and a series of amendments passed in 1939 would help move the program toward just such a wealth transfer program. They would also change the handout formula to make Social Security more redistributive *within* a generational cohort. Similarly, the amendments expanded beneficiaries to include the survivors of active and retired employees and dependents of retired workers.

As the 1930s drew to a close, FDR's signature achievement had taken shape, had passed constitutional muster, and was ready to start dispensing handouts. Its once precarious existence was beginning to seem more and more secure. More was to come. "As benefits expanded," notes historian W. Andrew Achenbaum, "so did pressure for more and more growth [of the Social Security program]. This is exactly what the president intended."[123]

Social Security was both an end and a beginning. Although its architects vehemently denied it, the Act and its 1939 amendments signaled the end of the self-reliant society, in which a person's wealth belonged to him, and the beginning of the entitlement state. Never before had the government been able to seize people's wealth on so grand a scale. It would help change the character of the U.S. government forever.

What was the ultimate policy goal of the entitlement statists? They were generally vague on this point, but in 1944, FDR made their intentions startlingly clear when he announced his goal of establishing a Second Bill of Rights.

> This Republic had its beginning, and grew to its present strength, under the protection of certain inalienable political rights—among them the right of free speech, free press, free worship, trial by jury, freedom from unreasonable searches and seizures. They were our rights to life and liberty.
>
> As our Nation has grown in size and stature, howev-

er—as our industrial economy expanded—these political rights proved inadequate to assure us equality in the pursuit of happiness.[124]

What did "equality in the pursuit of happiness" require? What new "rights" did the entitlement statists want to create? Said FDR:

- The right to a useful and remunerative job in the industries or shops or farms or mines of the Nation;
- The right to earn enough to provide adequate food and clothing and recreation;
- The right of every farmer to raise and sell his products at a return which will give him and his family a decent living;
- The right of every businessman, large and small, to trade in an atmosphere of freedom from unfair competition and domination by monopolies at home or abroad;
- The right of every family to a decent home;
- The right to adequate medical care and the opportunity to achieve and enjoy good health;
- The right to adequate protection from the economic fears of old age, sickness, accident, and unemployment;
- The right to a good education.[125]

The question few people asked was: If the government is going to guarantee people's food, clothing, recreation, job, home, medical care, education, and old age—and seize enough wealth to pay for it all—just what would be left of Americans' liberty? What *limits* would remain on government? What area of life would remain untouched by the state?

FDR never had the chance to enact his grand vision. Future generations of entitlement statists did.

CHAPTER FOUR

The Era of Expansion (1940–1972)

On January 31, 1940, Ida May Fuller received the first monthly handout from Social Security. A new era had begun. Despite their early misgivings, Americans, who had been told that they had earned their Social Security, started to embrace the program. The end of World War II brought a booming economy, and with payroll taxes low, few saw reason to complain.

For the entitlement statists, the next several decades would stand as a honeymoon period during which they happily played the part of Santa Claus. By front-loading handouts and hiding and postponing the costs, it truly seemed that they had the power to give people something for nothing. Thus Americans were presented with a seductive offer: Expand the entitlement state and you will be doing the moral thing—helping those in need—not at great cost, but in such a way that you yourself will benefit as well.

Americans still retained a respect for America's free-market roots, however, and there were limits to what the entitlement statists could get away with. In 1945, for instance, President Truman pushed to nationalize health insurance, but the effort collapsed. It would be another twenty years before Americans were ready to start socializing medicine.

Incremental efforts to expand Social Security were more successful. In 1950, Truman ushered in the first cost-of-living increase for Social Security (COLA), starting with a 77 percent increase over 1939 benefit levels. A few years later, disability benefits were included under the act. In 1961, early retirement became an option for Americans between sixty-two and sixty-four. Each new step seemed small in relation to what had come before. Why not raise benefits a bit? Why not cover a few more people? If taxes needed to be increased by a percent or two, that seemed a small price to pay. But while each step seemed small, the overall change was immense, and it produced a government whose size and scope few Americans in 1940 would have thought possible, let alone desirable. As historian Clarence Carson observed:

> The Welfare State became a fixture in the United States during the 1950s and 1960s. The dogmas of welfarism—that the government can and should provide for the material and intellectual well-being of the people, that it should control and direct the economy, and that the good life could be achieved in the framework of an all-caring government—were widely believed and acted on.[126]

Washington had declared that it had the power to intervene in the economy for the sake of any group that could plausibly claim to be "in need." In the decades following the Social Security Act, the results of this philosophy would spread like a disease throughout the government and the culture. The same ideas that had made Social Security a reality would start to make self-reliance a relic.

The Decline of Self-Reliance

As late as the Great Depression, Americans had a profound sense of pride and largely wanted nothing to do with government handouts. The common attitude, even in the depths of the Depression, was "I'd rather be dead and buried than be on the dole."[127] Accepting government aid was considered shameful—a last resort to be avoided at virtually any cost. FDR himself observed that "in this business of relief we are dealing with properly self-respecting Americans to whom a mere dole outrages every instinct of individual independence," which is one reason relief typically came in the form of make-work projects.[128]

This view of the dole had deep roots in the land of self-reliance. "Dependance begets subservience and venality, suffocates the germ of virtue, and prepares fit tools for the designs of ambition," Thomas Jefferson had said.[129] American immigrant Francis Grund observed in the late nineteenth century:

> I have never known a native American to ask for charity. No country in the world has such a small number of persons supported at the public expense. . . . An American, embarrassed by his pecuniary circumstances, can hardly be prevailed upon to ask or accept the assistance of his own relations; and will, in many instances, scorn to have recourse to his own parents.[130]

The entitlement statists regarded Americans' entrenched sense of pride and self-responsibility, not as a virtue, but as a problem that needed to be solved. One New Dealer complained that "established mores are undoubtedly too deeply embedded in the American spirit for the present to permit adequate relief to employable persons without requiring work in return." But, he added, "traditional attitudes toward 'getting something for nothing' are already undergoing change."[131] Thanks in large measure to Social Security and, more important, the spread of the ideas that *led* to Social Security, they were.

The shift in the American soul was subtle at first. Typically it was immigrants to America who were the first to notice it. Italian immigrant Mario Pei described how he had fled Europe—a land where "Young people did not dream of going into business for themselves" but of "a modest but safe government job"—to reach America, where, when he arrived in 1908, "the national ideal was not the obscure security of a government job, but the boundless opportunity that all Americans seemed to consider their birthright." But only a decade and a half after Social Security, Pei noted with sadness

> the growth of the familiar European-style government octopus, along with the vanishing of the American spirit of freedom and opportunity and its replacement by a breathless search for 'security' that is doomed to defeat in advance in a world where nothing, not even life itself, is secure.[132]

It was only a sample of what was to come. Nevertheless, it was clear by the 1950s that America had changed.

The symbol of the fifties worker was not the entrepreneurial hero of Horatio Alger, but "the Organization Man," as William Whyte's popular 1956 book put it. Earlier Americans had upheld thrift, hard work, individualism, and competitiveness. The new social ethic, Whyte wrote, could be summed up in three propositions: "a belief in the group as the source of creativity; a belief in 'belongingness' as the ultimate need of the individual; and a belief in the application of science to achieve that belongingness."[133] According to sociologist David Riesman, Americans had changed from self-reliant individualists into "outer-directed" social conformists.

Productive achievement, accordingly, was no longer seen as the central activity that made life exciting and meaningful. Instead,

Riesman wrote in 1960, young people of the era wanted to "build a nest . . . in contrast with the wish to build a fortune or a career which might have dominated" the concerns of young people "a generation earlier." Work "was primarily a way to earn a living, to find a place in the social order, and to meet nice or not-so-nice people."[134]

If self-reliance was a manifestation of individualism, the entitlement era saw a gradual shift away from individualism, self-reliance, and self-assertion to a dreary sort of conformity. Responsibility was not thrown out, but it was often recast in terms of responsibility to the family, the community, or society. More and more, life was not about making something of yourself and pursuing your own happiness, but of playing by the rules, doing your duty, supporting your family, and not getting into too much trouble along the way. In return for this conformity, you were told that you would be guaranteed—not opportunity, with its inherent risk—but security.

Social Security appealed to and encouraged this bland conventionality and "breathless search" for safety. If the goal of life was not to pursue *your* vision of life, but to color inside the lines, then Social Security provided a clear and comforting endpoint to strive for. Life was about going to school, getting a job, starting a family, paying your taxes, and then, when you hit sixty-five, retiring and spending your remaining years in quiet repose.

Throughout the forties and fifties, self-reliance continued to be held in high esteem, but it no longer served as the American ideal. It was not the primary yardstick by which men measured themselves and others. Slowly, "self-reliance" was becoming more rhetoric than reality. As Whyte observed:

> Collectivism? [Today's American] abhors it, and when he makes his ritualistic attack on Welfare Statism, it is in terms of . . . the sacredness of property, the enervating effect of security, the virtues of thrift, of hard work and independence. . . . He is not being hypocritical, only compulsive. He honestly wants to believe he follows the tenets he extols.[135]

Americans were drifting away from the self-reliant society, in philosophy and in fact—but without full awareness.[136]

As the moral status of self-reliance ebbed, the calls to be your brother's keeper grew louder and more strident. In self-reliant

America, one's primary moral obligation had been to support one-self if at all possible, and dependency had been seen as shameful. You *did* have a moral obligation to support others who needed your help, most Americans thought, but even there, you had a duty to be prudent about it. In the process of trying to help them, you must not hurt them by promoting dependency. Charity, said an 1835 report from Boston, "is abused, whenever it ministers in any way to a neglect of forethought and providence."[137] The goal of charity was to make charity unnecessary: to help people move from dependency to inde-pendence. When in doubt, you were to err on the side of supporting them too little.

By the early 1960s, however, the focus on supporting oneself was deemphasized, and the moral spotlight was put on the urgent neces-sity to serve those in need. Was there a risk of promoting dependency? Perhaps, but if those in need had a right to be kept then it was better to err on the side of providing "too much" financial support—it would be cruel and mean-spirited to withhold it. Those who tried to abide by the old philosophy, which said that the goal of charity was to make the recipients independent, were denounced. The goal, they were told, was to serve people's needs—period. Need was an entitlement, and you as the giver had no business imposing *your* views on the recipient, including your view that independence was superior to dependence, or that some were "deserving" while others were not.[138]

Most Americans, to be sure, did not want to see themselves as on the dole. They accepted that they were their brother's keeper—they recoiled at the idea of being one of the kept, which is one reason why the entitlement statists still insisted that Social Security was not a welfare program. But the status of those who *were* on the dole was changing. They were no longer pure objects of pity. Those "in need" were increasingly seen as *morally superior* to the individual who had made something of his life. The source of their need was irrelevant—whether it was through an unlucky accident or their own bad choices, their need entitled them to compassion and to other people's wealth. If, on the other hand, an individual succeeded at making something of himself, he gave up any claim either to compassion or to his wealth—the more he achieved, the more he owed to those in need. 'Twas nobler to be the kept than the keeper.

As the entitlement statists' demands for wealth redistribution in the name of being "your brother's keeper" became louder and louder, the incompatibility of self-reliance and self-sacrifice was becoming more apparent. If it had seemed that the culture could hold up both self-responsibility and responsibility for others as moral ideals, it was starting to become clear that it was one or the other. The only question was, which side would win?

As America entered the 1960s, two things were obvious: The entitlement state was growing and the society of self-reliance was transforming. Things were about to come to a head.

The Not-So-Great Society

The climax of the Age of Expansion came during the 1960s. It was during this decade that Americans saw the full flowering of the entitlement state Social Security had created. Most of these developments are beyond the scope of this work, but a few observations are in order.

As for Social Security proper, it continued to expand. When Wilbur Cohen proposed to President Lyndon B. Johnson that handouts be increased by 10 percent, Johnson responded, "Come on, Wilbur, you can do better than that." The president ended up proposing a 15 percent increase in handouts in 1967; Congress decided that was too generous and knocked it down to 13, while raising payroll taxes and increasing the cap on taxable earnings. Social Security had originally been sold as *security*—as a "floor of protection," to be supplemented by private savings and private pensions. The entitlement statists, it seemed, had bigger plans.[139]

It was also during this time that the entitlement statists started cautiously emphasizing Social Security's alleged impact on poverty. Not wanting to openly admit that Social Security was an entitlement designed to give people rewards on the basis of their need, they stressed, in the words of then Social Security Commissioner Robert Ball, that its "objective is not solely the abolition of poverty, but in its operation it does prevent poverty. It can be used much more effectively for this purpose."[140] According to Achenbaum:

> Such a restatement of goals echoed broader intellectual and political currents influencing national policy after 1960, even though social security was not conspicuous in the front ranks of the battle to extirpate poverty.[141]

What were those "broader intellectual and political currents"? Beginning with John F. Kennedy and accelerating under Lyndon B.

Johnson, the government declared war on poverty. Ignoring the fact that capitalism had already eradicated absolute poverty from America during the nineteenth and early twentieth centuries, the entitlement statists now argued that it was *relative* poverty that had to be fought through a laundry list of interventionist and redistributive measures known collectively as "the Great Society." With the notable exception of Medicare, most of these would be undisguised welfare measures, although to be sure Johnson professed that his intention was to give people a hand up, not a handout. By vastly expanding the entitlement state today, he said, it would become unnecessary tomorrow.

The centerpiece of the Great Society was the passage of Medicare and Medicaid in 1965. Both of these programs were created as amendments to the Social Security Act (Titles XVIII and XIX, respectively). Medicaid was a means-tested health welfare program. Medicare was modeled on Social Security's retirement scheme; it was not means-tested, but was funded through its own tax, and marketed to the public as "social insurance."

The entitlement statists had had their eyes on the health care system from the start. Along with unemployment, disability, and old age, sickness was one of the key areas in which they believed the government was obliged to ensure that people's unfulfilled needs were met. But Americans were wary of the government gaining control over their health care—it seemed a radical departure from the founding ideals.

Besides, it was not obvious to most that there was a problem in health care that needed to be solved.[142] Most elderly people were able to get the health care they needed. A *growing* number (more than half by 1960) carried insurance, while the others paid out of pocket, relied on friends and family, or turned to private charity. The entitlement statists denied all that or, when forced to concede that elderly Americans were receiving care, objected to the "indignity" of them having to ask for charity. The market, they said, was making these people dependent: We must make them self-reliant through a government program.[143]

It was the Social Security argument all over again. The free market had failed, people were in need, and society could help them at little cost. Economically, the entitlement statists said, we would be spending an almost trivial amount; ethically, we would be encouraging self-reliance, not sacrificing it; politically, we would be improving the free market by smoothing out its rough edges, not eliminating it. Under the circumstances, who could object? Only the callous, cold-hearted, and mean-spirited. When many doctors did object, saying that they had no desire to practice medicine under the control of the state, they were brushed aside as greedy reactionaries and told that the government would merely be paying bills, not interfering with how doctors and hospitals ran their practices. (Within a few years costs would skyrocket and, as Social Security commissioner and architect of Medicare Robert Ball would later admit, "We did have to interfere."[144])

Although Medicare and Medicaid would have enduring consequences for the country, some very public failures would cause the larger War on Poverty to implode.

The only intention the architects of the War on Poverty may fairly lay claim to was the desire to spend as much money as fast as possible on any program that could half-plausibly be described as having to do with poverty. That alone entitled them to moral righteousness and consigned their opponents to the sewers of depravity. As then Congressman William Windall observed, "Anybody who gets up and speaks against a slogan like ['War on Poverty'] is considered automatically a man without a heart, without humanitarianism, without any concern for the people who are the underprivileged."[145]

Unsurprisingly, the vast majority of the programs that emerged from this spending frenzy were marred by fraud and corruption. Perhaps most troubling were the stories that emerged from the Job Corps program. Formed to train "disadvantaged" inner-city youths, the Job Corps ended up enrolling thousands of dropouts, hoodlums, and criminals—many who used the time away from home to drink, fight, vandalize, get high, and riot. As for the "training," a visitor to one of the training sites observed that "half the kids were sleeping, the other half were indifferent and teachers were droning on and on with no involvement."[146]

Studies would eventually show that Jobs Corps applicants who did not end up enrolling in the program had *higher* rates of employment than those who graduated from the program.[147] The cost per enrollee, meanwhile, was between $10,000 and $40,000 in 1968 dollars (at a time when the median household income was $6,673): Such was the price that struggling, self-responsible Americans were forced to pay to "fight poverty." As one woman at the time told her Congressman:

How can I possibly pay taxes to support people in the

Jobs Corps centers at $13,000 a year? Our total income is $6,000 a year, and we have three children. We had hoped that we would be able to send our three children to college. Instead of that you are passing a program in the Congress of the United States which says that I am to pay taxes to support one person at $13,000 a year.[148]

The death knell of the War on Poverty was a new movement it helped encourage: the welfare rights movement. The traditional view of welfare, as Ronald Reagan put it in 1967, was that "There is no humanity or charity in destroying self-reliance, dignity, and self-respect."[149] But Johnson's Office of Economic Opportunity poured funding into the laps of advocates of what the *New York Times* called "a new philosophy of social welfare," which "seeks to establish the status of welfare benefits as rights, based on the notion that everyone is entitled to a share of the common wealth."[150] These activists wanted to subvert people's longstanding view that going on the dole was shameful. At the time, many of those eligible for welfare handouts still refused to accept them out of a sense of pride and individual responsibility. The "welfare rights" activists declared war on this attitude.

The most visible of these activists was the National Welfare Rights Organization. The NWRO was established in 1966 as the brainchild of two professors of social work at Columbia University, Frances Fox Piven and Richard Cloward, and was headed by black organizer George Wiley. Its goal was, in Marvin Olasky's words, "convincing welfare recipients that the fault lay in the stars ('systemic pathologies') rather than themselves." The NWRO went into poor communities and evangelized for welfare. As Olasky observes:

The NWRO proved successful in its immediate objectives. In its first four years an estimated 100,000 welfare recipients were organized and trained to demand payments, not ask for them. Observers at organizing meetings were struck by how welfare mothers came to them with a sense that welfare should be avoided, but "Wiley's constant repetition of the word *rights* got through to the women." *Time* quoted welfare mother and leader Mrs. Johnnie Tillmon as saying that the organization's goal was "everybody get what's coming to them. Everybody is entitled."[151]

As we shall see, this philosophy of entitlement would have a lasting impact on poor communities. But NWRO's activities as well as its belligerent demands for vastly larger welfare payments did much to discredit the War on Poverty in the eyes of the American public. It was too much, too soon. Despite all the confusions surrounding self-reliance, despite Americans' growing belief in the propriety of wealth redistribution, the open proclamation of entitlement was damning. The welfare rights movement imploded and in 1975 NWRO shut its doors.

The Entitlement State's War on the Poor

The effects of the War on Poverty on America's culture of self-reliance were devastating. Hardest hit were low-income communities. In the era before entitlements, there were poor communities, but for the most part they were not impoverished. Their inhabitants had little money, but they had a strong sense of pride and ambition—they were not what we would describe today as "underclass." A 1907 housing report on poor Polish immigrants in Baltimore observes, for example:

> A remembered Saturday evening inspection of five apartments in a house [on] Thames Street, with their whitened floors and shining cook stoves, with the dishes gleaming on the neatly ordered shelves, the piles of clean clothing laid out for Sunday, and the general atmosphere of preparation for the Sabbath, suggested standards that would not have disgraced a Puritan housekeeper.[152]

The existence of poverty without a *culture* of poverty wasn't unique to immigrants. Throughout the first half of the twentieth century, poor black communities were typically filled with two-parent households, vibrant business districts, and clean, safe streets. As economist Walter Williams notes of his childhood in a poor, predominantly black area of North Philadelphia:

> Graffiti and wanton property destruction were unthinkable. The closest thing to graffiti was the use of chalk to draw blocks on the pavement to play hopscotch. . . . Many families never locked their doors until late at night, after everyone was home. When people visited, they'd simply knock on the door and let themselves in.[153]

In the era of the entitlement state, we're seeing a rise of a *culture* of poverty.

Poverty had been declining steadily for years before the entitlement statists declared war on it, and it was only once their "War on Poverty" started spending trillions of dollars to end poverty that the poverty rate *stopped* declining. According to economists James Gwartney and Thomas S. McCaleb:

> By 1965 only 13.9 percent of American families were officially classified as poor, down from 32 percent in 1947 and 18.5 percent in 1959. Thus, in less than a generation economic progress had cut the overall poverty rate in half. Moreover . . . the poverty rate declined steadily in all age groups. Among the elderly, the poverty rate fell from 57 percent in 1947 to 22.8 percent in 1965. For youthful families, those headed by an individual under age 25, the poverty rate fell from 45 percent in 1947 to 26.9 percent in 1959 and to 19.4 percent in 1965. The pattern for families in the prime working-age groups is similar.[154]

The entitlement statists were not fazed in the least by these facts. Their aim was not to end dependency, but to end the *stigma* of dependency. Before the 1960s, writes Olasky, "the public dole was humiliation, but thereafter young men were told" by entitlement statists "that shining shoes was demeaning, and that accepting government subsidy meant a person 'could at least keep his dignity.'"[155] The goal, according to entitlement statist Richard Elman, was to "make dependency legitimate" so that recipients could "consume with integrity."[156] If the work ethic had once represented the idealization of self-reliance, then this campaign represented the idealization of dependency.[157]

How did the entitlement statists attempt to "make dependency legitimate"?

Ideologically, they preached the notion that individuals are helpless and therefore not responsible for their lives and behavior. Dependency, then, didn't reflect a moral failure on the part of the individual, but on the part of society. Society hadn't given you the education, or opportunity, or income, or intelligence, or work ethic, or moral character to keep you from loafing on your couch or drinking yourself into oblivion or resorting to a life of crime. The messier your life, the greater your right to demand recompense from society.

Economically, the entitlement state subsidized dependency and irresponsibility. Laziness got you a check that was likely larger than, say, the one earned by the poor immigrant who labored for twelve hours a day mowing lawns. Young thugs were in effect being paid by the government to hang around on street corners, hassling law-abiding citizens who still wanted to make something of their lives.

A new culture emerged. Whereas members of these communities had once been poor but proud, aspiring to build a better life through education and hard work, the desire to lift oneself out poverty was increasingly looked down upon. After all, if your next door neighbor could rise by his own bootstraps despite hardship, what did your failure to do so say about you? The result was that those who tried to better themselves—through education or entry-level jobs—were frequently mocked as sellouts, suckers, or even traitors to their race.

So began a decline in poor communities. "Today's urban poor," notes historian Thomas Sugrue, "are increasingly marginal participants in the urban labor market, entrapped in pockets of poverty that have little precedent in the nineteenth-century city."[158] Where ambition, achievement, and self-reliance are no longer nourished and where productive work no longer occupies the time of a significant number of people, what replaces them? Every sort of escape, from promiscuous sex to drug and alcohol abuse to gambling to violent crime. If you kill individual responsibility, irresponsibility flourishes.[159]

The Age of Expansion Comes to a Close

Much of the Great Society was viewed as a failure, but no small part of it endured. Medicare and Medicaid would grow enormously, welfare rolls were permanently increased, and the view of the dole as shameful was virtually extinguished—not only among recipients, but to a great extent among the public at large.

As for Social Security, its reputation remained pristine among both Democrats and Republicans. Nixon, for instance, expanded the program once again in 1972, signing into law the biggest increase, in terms of real dollars, in Social Security's history: a 20 percent rise in spending, coupled with new, automatic cost-of-living adjustments to keep up with inflation. The amendments included other changes, such as a new Supplemental Security Income (SSI) program to support low-income elderly Americans. "By the end of 1972," writes Achenbaum, every major idea that the 1935 Committee on Economic Security had considered for social security had been enacted. As its creators had hoped, coverage under social security was nearly universal. The proportion of Americans eligible for Title II [retirement] benefits had risen from 20 percent to 93 percent between 1941 and 1974; those over seventy-five had been entitled to government benefits for more than a decade. Furthermore, periodic increases in average monthly social security checks after 1950, passage of the SSI program, and the indexing of Title II benefits can all be interpreted as attempts to reduce the vulnerability of the elderly to inflation, thereby advancing their economic "freedom." Average monthly benefits for retired workers rose to $207 by the end of 1975. This increase was significant in terms of purchasing power; mid-1970s beneficiaries got roughly 40 percent more than their counterparts a decade earlier. Supporters claimed that disability insurance, Medicare, and Medicaid were the first victories in a thirty-year struggle to enact some sort of national health plan under the aegis of social insurance. The adoption of a wide range of community services and outreach programs was clearly consonant with principles that can be traced back to the New Deal.[160]

The entitlement statists were far from satisfied. But they would encounter a problem that would put an end to Social Security's honeymoon period. As the government's power over the economy ballooned, the economic prosperity the statists promised began to crumble and put the government's ability to provide more handouts in jeopardy. These economic troubles would open their programs to attack. Even the "third rail," Social Security, would become vulnerable.

CHAPTER FIVE

Social Security in Crisis (1972–Today)

What had made Social Security resemble "the greatest Ponzi game ever contrived"—at least in the eyes of its supporters—was the fact that people could receive in handouts far more than they ever paid in taxes, thanks to a growing workforce and a growing economy. Social Security's defenders had dismissed earlier concerns that those conditions might not hold up indefinitely. By the mid-to-late 1970s, they could no longer dismiss them.

In the earliest days of Social Security, there had been forty workers for every retiree. In 1950, the ratio was smaller but still impressive: 16.5:1. But by the close of the 1970s, there were only 3.3 workers to carry the burden for each retiree.[161] A second budget buster was "stagflation." High 1970s inflation meant that benefits would grow faster than expected, but declining productivity and employment rates meant that FICA tax revenues would be far less than expected. For example, the 1977 Social Security Board of Trustees report projected that over five years inflation would total 28.2 percent—it actually totaled 60 percent. It projected that real wages would increase 12.9 percent—they actually *declined* by 6.9 percent. It projected unemployment would average 5.9 percent—it actually averaged 6.7 percent.[162]

To make matters worse, the 1972 amendments had contained one of the greatest bloopers in all of American history. In rewriting the Social Security benefit formula, Congress had mistakenly double-indexed the Social Security benefits paid to new retirees. As Social Security expert Charles Blahous explains:

> These benefits were effectively indexed (meaning adjusted each year) both for wage growth *and* for price inflation. As a result, benefit levels began to grow so drastically that had this continued, retirees on Social Security would ultimately have received more money for not working than they had ever been paid for working. This rate of benefit growth vastly exceeded congressional intent as well as what was reasonably affordable.[163]

Yet even after correcting the botched 1972 formula in 1977, insolvency loomed. By the time Ronald Reagan took office in 1981, Social Security's financial straits could no longer be ignored.

The Swing to the Right

The 1970s had seen not only a shift in the financial health of Social Security but an ideological shift in the thinking of Americans. Since the New Deal, the country had been moving in the direction of greater government control over the economy, but not everyone supported this trend. There existed a diverse group intellectuals on the right who were working to stop the country's decline.

This group included free-market-leaning economists, such as F. A. Hayek and Milton Friedman; conservative and neoconservative thinkers such as William F. Buckley and Irving Kristol; and novelist-philosopher Ayn Rand, whose 1957 novel *Atlas Shrugged* had become one of the best-selling pro-capitalist works in history.

When, during the 1970s, things became so bad economically and culturally that they could not be ignored, Americans were roused. They were looking for an alternative, one that would rescue the economy and resuscitate the American spirit. But *where* should they head? What specific ideas and policies should they adopt? And why were these good and proper? On these points there was no consensus.

Rand argued that the only moral solution was to jettison the entire regulatory-entitlement state and establish complete, unregulated, uncontrolled, laissez-faire capitalism. But for that to happen, Rand said, an even more radical change would be required: American culture would have to transform. Americans would have to embrace the ideals of the self-reliant society, but in an unadulterated form—one that jettisoned every trace of the notion that "you are your brother's keeper." That notion, Rand held, could *not* be reconciled with the conviction that each individual is an end in himself, not a means to the ends of others. It was one or the other.

Rand's critique of the entitlement state, then, went deeper than politics. It challenged the moral premises of entitlement. You are *not* your brother's keeper, Rand argued. You have a right to exist for your own sake, neither sacrificing yourself for others nor others to yourself. The government's only moral function was to protect that right. Helping others was a personal matter each individual must be free to decide for himself—not a social question.

> If a man speculates on what "society" should do for the
> poor, he accepts thereby the collectivist premise that
> men's lives belong to society and that *he*, as a member of
> society, has the right to dispose of them, to set their goals
> or to plan the "distribution" of their efforts.[164]

According to Rand, the entitlement statist method was to advocate a grand-scale public goal that, out of context, was desirable—e.g.,
that poor people have more money or that the elderly should have
health care—and then to ignore and evade the *means*.

> *Out of context*, such a goal can usually be shown to be
> desirable; it has to be public, because the *costs* are not to
> be earned, but to be expropriated; and a dense patch of
> venomous fog has to shroud the issue of *means*—because
> the means are to be human *lives*.[165]

Hayek, Friedman, and sundry conservatives dismissed the idea that
so radical a solution as laissez-faire capitalism was necessary or even
desirable. Economically, they said, the country needed merely to cut
taxes, trim regulations, and lower spending. Some advocated doing away
with entitlements, although this was by no means universal, especially
among conservatives.[166]

In truth, the conservative view was murky at best. Conservatives
agreed with the left that man is his brother's keeper and has a duty to
selflessly serve others, but they also railed against dependency. They
damned wealth redistribution, but they smeared those like Rand who
objected to the idea of a tax-financed "safety net." They labeled the
Great Society a travesty, but they hailed the New Deal as an American
triumph. As for Social Security, they bought into the fiction that it
was a "social insurance" program providing "earned benefits," and
wished only to make it economically sustainable. To the extent theirs
approached a coherent position, it amounted to the view that the entitlement state was okay so long as it wasn't "too big" and its incentives
weren't "too perverse."

Although Rand's books had helped move the country to the right
and make questioning the entitlement state acceptable, when it came
time for intellectual and political leadership, it was the conservatives
to whom the public turned.

Ronald Reagan Saves Social Security

Ronald Reagan is considered one of the great champions of capitalism and has been reviled by opponents for his antagonism toward the entitlement state. There is no basis for this in historical fact. Reagan was adamant that the government must provide a "safety net" (a term he coined), and under his tenure, the entitlement state would not shrink, but grow—more slowly than under previous administrations perhaps, but grow all the same.

When it came to Social Security, Reagan had a unique opportunity. Even the entitlement statists understood that the program could not possibly continue in its current form. If nothing were done to make Social Security viable, it would collapse. This gave the right immense leverage.

Republicans could have pointed out that Social Security's inability to pay its bills proved once and for all that it was not a savings program distributing earned benefits but a redistribution scheme that allowed each generation to loot the next. They could have explained that the only way to "rescue" the system would be to place increasingly onerous burdens on younger (and not-yet-born) Americans, robbing them of many of their hopes and dreams. They could have condemned Social Security as an enemy of American self-reliance and capitalism and put the entitlement statists on the defensive. Reagan never even tried. In 1981, he appointed a commission to *save* Social Security.

Reagan's failure should not be surprising. The truth was that by this time virtually all Americans regarded the entitlement state as a morally indispensable part of government's job. Although the modern political right still paid lip service to the ideal of self-reliance, both Reagan and his fellow conservatives agreed with the basic principle behind the entitlement state: that a person's need entitled him to other people's wealth. They agreed that an America without an entitlement state would be cruel and harsh. Did they want the entitlement state to be smaller? To cost less? To cause less harm? In theory yes, but they were terrified of making any specific proposals to rein in entitlements. How could they possibly answer the charge they were greedy tools of the rich, eager to throw Grandma off a cliff?

Reagan's Social Security Commission would broker a compromise between Republicans and Democrats that would address Social Security's financial troubles by kicking the can down the road. In essence, the 1983 deal aimed to stave off Social Security's day of reckoning by mildly reducing handouts over time, primarily by slowly raising the retirement age, and by accelerating payroll tax increases.

One thing was now clear. Social Security wasn't secure. Its promise of a guaranteed income was empty. The program's risks, conclude Social Security experts Sylvester Schieber and John Shoven,

> are considerable. Think about it—taxes were raised and benefits cut in 1977. Taxes were raised and future benefits cut in 1983. Now [in 1999] we see that the system has a large long-term deficit. Unless we consider changing its very structure, we will have no choice but to raise taxes and cut benefits once again. . . . [T]he current program is proving very risky for young participants, given that the terms offered continue to deteriorate. If a private insurance policy kept raising the premiums and lowering the benefits, one would not hesitate to call it a risky contract. The same should be true for Social Security.[167]

Whatever the case, the 1983 deal did save Social Security from imminent insolvency, but it quickly became clear that the shortfall would re-emerge in the first part of the twenty-first century once the program again started handing out more than it received in payroll taxes. When precisely would this happen? What would the effects be? And how easy would it be to fix? That all depended on one's view of the trust fund.

The 1983 reforms sought to balance Social Security revenues and outlays *on average* for seventy-five years. It accomplished this by creating huge trust fund surpluses in the first thirty years, and then assuming that the fund could be used to cover the rising outlays that followed. If the trust fund consisted of real savings, then that might have been plausible. It would be similar to an individual building up a 401(k) when he's young, and living off the income when he retired. But the trust fund did not in fact represent genuine savings.

The Social Security "surplus" was not being saved—it was being spent on other government programs in exchange for IOUs in the form of government bonds. Once Social Security started handing out more than it was taking in from payroll taxes, it would have to redeem those bonds. How? Ultimately, by taxing Americans more and more. The best analogy for Social Security's trust fund is to think of parents who set aside their child's college fund in a jar, but who periodically "borrow" from the jar whenever they want to go on vacation or eat a fancy meal, replacing the cash with an IOU. By the time the child is ready to go to college, the jar full of IOUs will not do a thing to help the parents to pay for their child's schooling. So it is for Social Security's trust fund.[168]

In a 1998 speech at Georgetown University, President Bill Clinton spelled out the implications with admirable candor:

> This fiscal crisis in Social Security affects every generation. We now know that [Social Security] is fine for another few decades. But if it gets in trouble and we don't deal with it, then it not only affects the generation of the baby boomers and whether they'll have enough to live on when they retire, it raises the question of whether they will have enough to live on by unfairly burdening their children and, therefore, unfairly burdening their children's ability to raise their grandchildren. That would be unconscionable, especially since, if you move now, we can do less and have a bigger impact. . . .
>
> It's very important you understand this. . . . If you don't do anything, one of two things will happen—either it will go broke and you won't ever get it; or if we wait too long to fix it, the burden on society of taking care of our [baby boom] generation's Social Security obligations will lower your income and lower your ability to take care of your children to a degree most of us who are your parents think would be horribly wrong and unfair to you and unfair to the future prospects of the United States. . . .
>
> Today, we're actually taking in a lot more money from Social Security taxes enacted in 1983 than we're spending out. Because we've run deficits, none of that money has been saved for Social Security. . . .
>
> And if nothing is done by 2029, there will be a deficit in the Social Security trust fund, which will either require—if you just wait until then—a huge tax increase in the payroll tax, or just about a 25 percent cut in Social Security benefits.[169]

Clinton himself mulled over establishing private Social Security accounts in the hopes they would enable the program to achieve actual savings, but any such plans were derailed by his impeachment troubles.[170]

Bush, Obama, and Twenty-First-Century Entitlement Statism

It was in this context that President George W. Bush attempted to tackle Social Security's financial troubles in the first half of the 2000s. While ruling out any cuts or changes to Social Security for retirees or near-retirees, he advocated individually controlled, voluntary private accounts for young people. Whatever the flaws of Bush's approach, it was not his actual approach that was attacked. Instead, opponents charged that he wanted to cut benefits for current retirees, and to "privatize" all of Social Security. As Charles Blahous puts it, Bush's critics were "essentially inventing a Social Security plan, attributing it to [Bush], and trumpeting its specific adverse effects."[171] Bush tried twice to push for Social Security reform during his presidency. Both times he failed.

The entitlement statists saw Bush as secretly wanting to destroy Social Security. They were wrong. Bush was sincere about wanting to, in his words, "strengthen and save Social Security for generations to come," going so far as to praise FDR's program as "an incredible achievement."[172] George W. Bush was not a free market champion who sought to appease entitlement statists—Bush *was* an entitlement statist. He actively fought to defend and expand the entitlement state.

This was the meaning of Bush's "compassionate conservatism," with its clear implication that old-style conservatism's ambivalence toward the entitlement state was "uncompassionate." Bush embraced the entitlement state without reservation—through and through, and all the way down. "When somebody hurts, the government has got to move," he said.[173] He sought, with a genuine eagerness, not to rein in entitlements but to expand them, above all in the areas of housing and health care. In housing, Bush doubled down on Clinton-era policies to promote homeownership among low-income Americans. In health care, Bush and a Republican Congress created the largest new entitlement since Lyndon Johnson, the 2003 prescription drug entitlement. Add it all up and you get the biggest spender in American history up to that point: Bush was the first president to propose a $2 trillion budget (2002) and the first to propose a $3 trillion budget (2008).

Nevertheless, Bush's critics accused him of "cowboy capitalism" and the reputation, undeserved as it was, stuck. By the time he left office, Bush had come to symbolize in the public's mind the failure of free-market policies and the need for change.

Barack Obama swept into office promising change. But when it came to entitlements, the new president made perhaps a dime's worth of difference in practice. Whereas Bush vowed to grow the entitlement state while lowering taxes, Obama pretended he could grow it while only raising taxes on "the rich." Whereas Bush expanded the entitlement state during an economic boom, artificial though it may have been, Obama expanded the entitlement state at a time when the country had gone bust.

There was only one respect in which Obama showed himself to be fundamentally different from his predecessor. Bush was motivated to expand the entitlement state by a sense of Christian duty; Obama was motivated by a hatred of self-reliance.

Obama represents the climax of entitlement statism in America. Although he gives a nod to self-reliance when it suits his purposes—entitlements, he said, promote "self-reliance and individual initiative" by giving everyone "a fair shot"[174]—his soul was on full display when he denied the self-reliant man ("You didn't build that") and mocked the self-reliant society as one that left people alone and abandoned: "If you lose your job you're on your own, if you get sick, you're on your own," he said, as if there were no possible sources of help other than government.[175] He did not hesitate to put our money where his mouth is: The Obama administration devoted immense resources to expanding the entitlement state in the face of public resistance. "One in seven Americans are on food stamps," the *Daily Caller* reported in 2012, "but the government is pushing to enroll more—in many instances working to overcome Americans' 'pride,' self-reliance or failure to see a need."[176] Obama's aim is to extinguish the last vestiges of the self-reliant society from America. Hence the centerpiece of his presidency: ObamaCare.

Upon signing the Social Security Act of 1935 FDR had declared that it was "a cornerstone in a structure which is being built but . . . is by no means complete."[177] It would not be complete until the government guaranteed that Americans had a "right to adequate medical care and the opportunity to achieve and enjoy good health."[178] FDR was unable to complete the structure—he lacked the political support for government to take over health care. Barack Obama was determined to finish what his progenitor had started.

To achieve his goal of imposing ObamaCare on the nation that had accepted RooseveltCare, Obama followed FDR's playbook to the letter:

- Social Security was sold on the premise that people must be forced to save for retirement; ObamaCare would be sold on the premise that people must be forced to buy health insurance.

- The New Dealers had smeared opponents of Social Security as cold-hearted enemies of the old; Obama's supporters would smear opponents of ObamaCare as cold-hearted enemies of the sick.
- FDR claimed that he was saving capitalism by addressing its failings; Obama would claim that he was saving private health insurance by addressing its failings.
- FDR found it necessary to hide the true cost of Social Security from the public; Obama had the audacity to sell ObamaCare as a means of lowering health care costs.
- The New Dealers took careful pains to make sure the Supreme Court would rule Social Security constitutional; Obama and his supporters knew that there was virtually nothing today's Supreme Court would stop the government from doing. Asked by the press which part of the Constitution gave Congress the power to compel Americans to buy health insurance, House Speaker Nancy Pelosi replied, "Are you serious?"[179]

The opponents of ObamaCare, it turned out, would largely follow the playbook of their predecessors as well. Social Security's opponents had granted the nobility of the program's goals and bickered over its details. They did not object to its moral essence—state control over how the individual plans for his old age—but to its costs. Their proposed alternative was to offer Social Security-lite, in the form of a guaranteed income to the elderly. They *did* scream that Social Security was socialism, but they could not defend that claim, and the charge was easily dismissed as over-the-top fear-mongering. Obama's opponents, it seemed, had learned nothing from history.

As for Social Security, Obama has mainly avoided the issue, which at this point is a political minefield for both sides. Obama's fellow entitlement statists, however, have made their position clear. Senator Elizabeth Warren declared that instead of reining in Social Security, we should *expand* it. She was criticized by left-wing wonk Ezra Klein for "not thinking big enough!"[180]

That is where we are today. Since its start, Social Security has spent more than $11.3 trillion dollars and taken in more than $13.8 trillion in taxes, with that $2.5 trillion surplus fueling the growth of other government programs. More than thirty million retirees currently receive benefits, totaling around $40 billion a month. The program as a whole pays out more than $55 billion each month.[181] And it is only one component of the burgeoning entitlement state it sparked—one that is now responsible for two-thirds of the government's nearly $4 trillion-plus budget, and growing. A majority of Americans now live in homes where someone receives entitlement handouts. As American Enterprise Institute scholar Nicholas Eberstadt notes, "total entitlement payouts on a real per capita basis have been growing twice as fast as per capita income over the past twenty years."[182]

Politically, not much is left of the social system crafted by the Founders. Which of our personal decisions does the government leave in our hands? Education? Employment? Housing? Health care? Retirement? Far from respecting the principle of self-reliance—which says that we have the freedom and the responsibility to plan our own lives—the government today is operating more and more on the principle of collectivism, which says that our lives are the property and responsibility of society.

What has the impact of the entitlement state and its collectivist philosophy been on the American culture? "The notion of a self," observed Tom Wolfe in a 1996 essay,

> who exercises self-discipline, postpones gratification, . . . stops short of aggression and criminal behavior—a self who can become more intelligent and lift itself to the very peaks of life by its own bootstraps through study, practice, perseverance, and refusal to give up in the face of great odds—this old-fashioned notion . . . of success through enterprise and true grit is already slipping away . . . . The peculiarly American faith in the power of the individual to transform himself from a helpless cypher into a giant among men . . . is now as moribund as the god for whom Nietzsche wrote an obituary in 1882.[183]

It's no mystery why we've seen this disintegration of personal responsibility. Responsibility flourishes in a society that preaches the virtue of responsibility, that rewards responsibility, that punishes irresponsibility, and in which the vast majority of citizens act as models of responsibility. That is not the world we live in today. The entitlement statists and the entitlement state deserve a considerable share of the blame.

A "something for nothing" philosophy is ultimately a philosophy that severs actions and consequences. The entitlement statists promised people paychecks without the need to work, retirement funds without the need to save and invest, charity without the need to ask people for their hard-earned money. They said not to worry about developing good habits and making good choices; the state would guarantee everyone good results. Americans were told, in effect, that thinking deeply about how to live was unnecessary. Whatever you needed would be provided for you, no need to worry about where the windfall would come from. Had people bothered to ask who was paying for their wrong choices the answer would have been: Those who made the right choices.

Thus the entitlement state and the entitlement philosophy have come together to help foster a growing *entitlement mentality*. This mentality exhibits a specific kind of irresponsibility: the righteous sense that one is to be supplied unearned rewards coupled with a defiant refusal to consider the source of those rewards—neither the individuals who are to produce them nor the political-economic system required to produce them. We see this mentality all around us today.

We see it when unwary Americans support ObamaCare in the belief it will provide them with "free" health care, and are shocked to learn that their insurance bill is higher than ever. We see it in fast food workers who demand a "living wage" far in excess of what their skills can justify, heedless of how this would harm their employer. We see it in the college students who demand forgiveness of their student loans, unconcerned with who would be forced to pick up their tab. We saw it during the housing boom, when Americans demanded loans for homes they could not afford. We saw it during the housing bust, when bankers demanded bailouts for deals they shouldn't have made.

And we see it in those card-carrying AARP members who protest any cut in their Social Security and Medicare benefits, even though most of them will receive hundreds of thousands of dollars more from the government than they ever paid in taxes—while their grandchildren are slated to pay hundreds of thousands more in taxes than they will ever receive in benefits.

Where Are We Going?

In their terrifying account of America's debt crisis, *The Clash of Generations*, Laurence Kotlikoff and Scott Burns argue that

> when individuals can't pay their bills, they are bankrupt. When companies can't pay their bills, they are bankrupt. And when countries, even those that print their own money and can still get foreigners to accept it, can't pay their bills, they are bankrupt. Thanks to six decades of incredibly profligate and irresponsible generational policy, we can declare, *The United States is bankrupt*.[184]

Examining the government's own data, Kotlikoff argues that as of 2013, our nation's debt stands not at the $17 trillion official figure but at an incredible $205 trillion in present value terms, the vast majority of which is a result of entitlement programs serving (mainly) the elderly: Social Security, Medicare, and Medicaid.[185] To make good on our promises of handouts, in other words, we would have to take $205 trillion *today* and invest it for eternity. The trouble is, we don't have $205 trillion lying around. That's more wealth than exists in the world.

The equation is simple. More Americans than ever are retiring, each retiree is consuming a greater amount of resources via government entitlement programs, and fewer American workers exist to shoulder that burden. If we don't do something to fix this mess soon, the entitlement state will bring about an economic crisis that could wreck the entire economy.

Kotlikoff and Burns argue that trying to parse out the costs of individual programs inevitably leads to underestimating their costs, thanks to government accounting gimmicks. But the government's own estimates of Social Security's costs are themselves troubling. According to the 2013 report from the Board of Trustees of the Federal Old-Age Survivors Insurance and Federal Disability Insurance Trust Funds, Social Security faces a shortfall of $23.1 trillion—50 percent larger than GDP.[186]

However, trying to isolate the cost of Social Security is of limited importance, even for our purposes. Social Security paved the way for entitlement programs such as Medicare and Medicaid, and it will not be reformed in any significant manner so long as those programs are viewed as sacrosanct. All of them are products of the same moral outlook, one that says that self-reliance is both impossible (we are incapable of making rational decisions) and immoral (our primary duty is to selflessly serve others). Either we question the whole entitlement state and the moral outlook that produced it, or we don't.

And if we don't, the economic consequences are dire. That $205 trillion gap constitutes 10 percent of the present value of all future GDP. To come up with that amount, the government would have to do far more than tinker with the entitlement state. It would have to raise *all* federal taxes by 54.8 percent immediately and forever. If we try to kick the can down the road twenty years, that number skyrockets to 65.3 percent.[187]

There are other possibilities, none of them good. One possible scenario is that the government will try to print money like mad in order to fulfill the promised handouts, sparking mass inflation or even hyperinflation. Another scenario is government default—on its debt, its entitlement commitments, or to some degree on both. The worst case, according to some economists, is that a default on government debt will take a heavy toll on credit markets, with the fallout dwarfing the 2008 financial crisis. Americans depending on Social Security and Medicare would be particularly hard hit, as their benefits stopped flowing.[188]

The entitlement state is in crisis. Either our political leaders will face the music and hit us with a tab so enormous that Americans will in all likelihood rebel—or they will bury their heads in the sand in the hopes that they will be dead before our day of reckoning arrives.

There is another option. We can use this as an opportunity to stop and reexamine the entitlement state—to question its necessity and morality. If we do, we can not only avoid disaster—we can create a freer, more prosperous, more moral America.

Now is the time, not to save the entitlement state, but to dismantle it.

The source of property rights is the law of causality. All property and all forms of wealth are produced by man's mind and labor. As you cannot have effects without causes, so you cannot have wealth without its source: without intelligence. You cannot force intelligence to work: those who're able to think, will not work under compulsion; those who will, won't produce much more than the price of the whip needed to keep them enslaved. You cannot obtain the products of a mind except on the owner's terms, by trade and by volitional consent. Any other policy of men toward man's property is the policy of criminals, no matter what their numbers. Criminals are savages who play it short-range and starve when their prey runs out— just as you're starving today, you who believed that crime could be 'practical' if your government decreed that robbery was legal and resistance to robbery illegal.

—Ayn Rand, *Atlas Shrugged*

CHAPTER SIX

Social Security vs. Self-Reliance

We've now heard the story of Social Security. We've seen that as Social Security and the entitlement state have grown, the self-reliant man and the self-reliant society have suffered. We've seen that Social Security replaced American capitalism with an entitlement state in which our property is not sacrosanct—in which pressure groups vie for the privilege of seizing what we earn, and in which, more and more, *need* rather than productive achievement is what entitles a person to wealth. At the same time, we've seen that the philosophy of entitlement has helped transform our culture. Fewer and fewer of our fellow citizens are taking responsibility for their own lives. Dependency now looms large in the land of independence.

It's time to render a verdict on RooseveltCare.

What is the case for Social Security? Supporters say that Social Security is a moral imperative because only it can provide elderly Americans with the economic security they need to face their golden years with dignity. An unwavering commitment to self-reliance, on this view, is impossible, since we all depend on society, and it is immoral, since the fact that we depend on society obligates us to give something back. To value the elderly is to defend old-age entitlements and their continued expansion. Anything less is cruelty to the aged.

What is the case against Social Security? What we require from society is not favors or handouts but the *freedom* to support our own lives through independent thought, productive effort, and voluntary cooperation with other self-supporting individuals—in a word, self-reliance. Self-reliance is both possible and necessary. Not only *can* human beings support themselves through independent thought and productive effort, but in the end, it is the *only* way they can support themselves. The true source of economic security is self-reliance and economic freedom—Social Security is immoral because it subverts both. It sabotages the virtues that enable us to survive, prosper, and enjoy our lives—and the social system that lets us exercise those virtues.

It's clear which side of this debate history comes down on. But it is vital that we make the lessons of history explicit. The notion that Social Security is a moral necessity is so deeply embedded that to excise it requires major intellectual surgery. We must examine the case for and against Social Security in detail—starting with the effects of Social Security on self-reliance.

Social Security: A Weapon of Mass Destruction

Self-reliance is about building a life for yourself—figuring out what you want from your days and years and then working to achieve it. At virtually every step, the pursuit of your hopes and dreams requires *money*. If self-reliance consists of supporting your life through productive work, then money is the instrument of self-reliance. Whether you want to buy a car or buy a home, see a movie or see the world, start a business or start a family, you need wealth to pursue your happiness. Every dollar you earn adds to your ability to get the most out of life. By seizing a sizeable and ever-growing portion of our income, the entitlement state makes self-reliance more and more difficult. Every dollar the government seizes comes at the expense of your hopes and dreams.

And oh, how many dollars it seizes.

Entitlement statists love to cite statistics claiming that without entitlements, our poverty rate would be far higher. Take away Social Security, they argue, and America's poverty rate rises from 16.1 to 24.4 percent. "Without Social Security, an additional 8.3 percent of Americans, or over 25 million more people, would fall below the SPM [Supplemental Poverty Measure] poverty threshold."[189] But these figures are meaningless, because they ignore the *costs* of the entitlement state.

How much does Social Security take from us? Right now its direct toll is 12.4 percent on the first $113,700 of your earnings. The median household income in the United States as of 2012 was $51,017.[190] For such a household, Social Security slashes its budget by $6,326. To put that into perspective, it means that for an entire month and a half, the household is working to pay for other people's retirement. We would think it monstrous if a boss demanded two hours of unpaid work—and yet we seem to have no problem with Social Security sentencing a family to over *250* hours of unpaid labor.

Even for relatively well-off Americans, the pain of losing 12.4 percent of their income should not be minimized. But think of what this does to young people who are just starting out in life. Six thousand dollars a year can sentence a person to living in a high-crime neighborhood, keep him from starting a family, or force him to stay at a dead-end job rather than following his dream to start a business. That is a travesty.

And that's just the direct annual cost of Social Security taxes. As heavy as it is, it is far from the whole story. The fact is that Social Security does not just "redistribute" wealth. It drastically reduces how much wealth is produced in the first place. It is not zero-sum—it is negative-sum.

The self-reliant society provided Americans with the greatest possible freedom and incentive to produce. The entitlement state curtails that freedom and dampens those incentives by taxing work and subsidizing non-work. Social Security, for instance, incentivizes enormously productive workers—workers with decades of knowledge and experience—to stop working years before they might have otherwise retired. (If you continue working and earning money after you apply for early benefits, your benefits are correspondingly reduced.)

At the same time, a substantial portion of the wealth redistributed by the entitlement state is taken out of the hands of people who would have saved and invested it, and put into the hands of people who consume it, while also obviating the *need* to save by promising to deliver unearned "benefits." America's national savings rate has declined from around 15 percent in 1950 to roughly *zero*.[191]

This is particularly damaging because it is savings and investment that maintain and increase a nation's standard of living over time. In the past, self-reliant Americans produced more than they consumed, investing the savings in things like more efficient factories, better machinery, and research and development, which spurred technological innovation. The result was that workers became more and more productive. The same human effort could produce an increasingly greater amount of wealth.

This—not the entitlement state—was the process responsible for Americans' rising standard of living. As workers produced more, they earned more—and the more they earned and saved, the more they could produce in the future, ad infinitum. Rising productivity was the cure for poverty and the path to prosperity. The entitlement statists took rising productivity for granted, denied that it helped poor people, and claimed Americans had only one option if they wanted to reduce poverty: force some people to work and labor for the sake of others.

But the entitlement state did not end poverty—it reduced prosperity. It had to. Poverty is not a distribution problem but a production problem. Entitlements don't increase production, but they do increase consumption. Wealth that would otherwise fund new factories or machinery (or maintenance of existing ones) instead goes to pay for Doritos, cell phones, tennis shoes, and the like. The overall result is to slow the rate at which we get richer and, ultimately, to strangle the productive capacity of the economy altogether.[192]

What has the entitlement state's war on capital accumulation meant for individual Americans? Laurence Kotlikoff and Scott Burns argue that the deterioration of American savings and investment is largely responsible for the troubling fact that real wages appear to have been virtually stagnant since 1964.

> [A]s our labor force grows in terms of the number of workers and their capabilities, there is an ever-growing shortage of capital per worker. The flip side of having capital become ever more scarce compared to labor (measured in terms of its productive capacity) is that labor becomes ever more abundant compared to capital. This leads to downward pressure on real wages in the marketplace.[193]

Developing this line of thinking, economist Edgar Browning estimates that, by creating bad incentives and redirecting spending from investment to consumption, the entitlement state

> *lowers the income of the average American by 25 percent.* Note that this does not refer to the direct tax burden of supporting these policies; the 25 percent loss is in before-tax income and is in addition to any taxes paid. . . . This is a huge total loss, more than $4 *trillion* annually.[194]

Social Security is by far the biggest villain in this story. According to Browning, "The average household . . . loses more than $12,000 from Social Security each year, and that is before they pay their Social Security taxes."[195]

It is a mistake, however, to think only in terms of dollars and cents. Social Security hasn't merely shrunk our incomes. It has left us less to buy with the dollars that remain. The entitlement state has been the silent killer of innovation, a point philosopher Harry Binswanger drives home:

> Imagine in 1980 a resident of California who is about to invest $5,000 in a new company called "Microsoft." But

at the last minute, he is conned by a Ponzi-scheme artist, a la Bernie Madoff, and he is convinced to give him the $5,000 instead. The con artist spends the money on consumption—whether his own or that of the "needy" is irrelevant—and he finds new suckers to get the money to pay the interest to the man who "invested" the $5,000. But nothing is actually invested; all the money is consumed.

Multiply that by 100 million households and continue it for 75 years and you can get a sense of the magnitude of the loss created by Social Security.

Of course Microsoft did obtain the investment funds (from IBM). What we cannot know is the other innovative firms that were not funded, and consequently the wondrous things that were not invented, not produced, and the wealth that is not there for anyone, old and young, to enjoy.[196]

And, *still*, we have understated the economic cost of Social Security. Because at the same time that it drained the pockets of productive Americans, and reduced their savings, and curtailed their productivity, and slowed technological progress, it did something else: It destroyed the purchasing power of the dollar. America's entitlement state unleashed *inflation*, as the government has essentially printed money to finance its enormous debts, debts driven by Social Security above all else.

But nothing is for free. Printing money led to relentless price increases and diluted the value of Americans' savings. What would have cost $108 in 1913 (the year the Federal Reserve was created) would cost *$2,422* by 2008.[197] The effect was to dilute the value of a person's life savings—and to make him less likely to save in the first place.

Finally, we must remember that Social Security is only one (albeit a major) component of the entitlement state. In 2010, entitlement spending at all levels of government totaled more than $2.2 trillion—more than the entire GDP of Italy. According to economist Nicholas Eberstadt, "the burden of all entitlement spending (federal, state, and local) amounted to over "$7,200 for every man, woman, and child in America. Scaled against a notional family of four, the average entitlements burden for that year alone would have approached $29,000."[198]

You might wonder at this point: If the entitlement state is so economically destructive, then how is it that America has become richer in the years since Social Security? The short answer is that we have grown richer *despite* entitlements, not because of them.

America's economic rise began well before the entitlement state was created, as capitalism unleashed the human and financial capital necessary to lift men out of pre-industrial poverty. Americans became rich because entrepreneurs and innovators created a new abundance, revolutionizing fields such as agriculture, textiles, energy, transportation, and communication.

After the entitlement state was created, it was the remaining elements of capitalism that enabled Americans to leverage that capital base during the mid-twentieth century to produce the greatest wave of mass prosperity the world had ever seen. In the wake of World War II, it was not entitlement statists who made us rich—it was men like Walmart founder Sam Walton, whose innovations allowed consumers to fill their homes with clothing, décor, and appliances that were once reserved for the rich.

The entitlement statists love to cite the 1950s as proof that high taxes and high government spending are compatible with high economic growth. But the truth of the matter is revealed by the fact that they do not take credit for the 1960s and 1970s, in which high taxes and even higher government spending led to economic catastrophe.

Whatever prosperity we have achieved and continue to achieve is a product of our remaining freedom and those self-reliant individuals who travel to places like Silicon Valley in the hopes of turning an idea into a fortune. And our prosperity is far, far less than what we would have achieved were the self-reliant society not undercut by entitlement.[199]

Small reductions in economic growth can have incredible impact over time. If, starting in 1870, economic growth had been just 1 percent lower each year than it was, our standard of living today would be lower than Mexico's, so while the full cost of Social Security is incalculable, we can say this: The entitlement state has made each of us far poorer than we would otherwise be. Any argument to the effect that, without the entitlement state, some group of recipients would be worse off is wholly false. It is plausible only because we cannot see how much better off we would have been had the country remained free. We hear, for instance, that poverty among the elderly has declined since the passage of Social Security. However, *all* self-reliant Americans would be far richer had capitalism been allowed to work and the entitlement state not consumed so much of their wealth.

It can't be stressed enough: The costs of the entitlement state include all of the benefits we *would* have reaped had we remained a self-reliant nation. This is true even though we cannot specify how incredible those benefits would have been. Imagine if America had been taken over by the Soviet Union seventy-five years ago. You might not be able to say precisely how much better off we would have been had we remained in a freer society. You would not know exactly how high our incomes would have risen. Nor would you know that we missed out on modern agriculture, personal computers, the Internet, cell phones, diaper genies, MRIs, new cancer- and AIDS-fighting medications, 3D printers, fracking technology, flat screen TVs, ebooks, and nanotechnology. You would not know to mourn the loss of Walmart, Target, Apple, Microsoft, Netflix, Virgin, Amazon, Zappos, FedEx, YouTube, and Google. Nevertheless, you would be able to say—to say *definitively*—that we would have been far, far better off had we not abandoned capitalism. Although the costs of the entitlement state are perhaps not quite so dramatic, the principle is the same.

The self-reliant society, to be sure, did not *guarantee* anyone money. This was not a cruel failure of the system. It was a recognition of the fact that money represents wealth—goods and services for which it can be exchanged—and this in turn presupposes that those goods and services have been produced. The government can print green pieces of paper at will—it cannot bring new *wealth* into existence by fiat. The government cannot guarantee anyone income—it can only help some people loot others. But in America's self-reliant era, many people recognized that "wealth redistribution"—whether in the form of illegal theft or legalized plunder—had no place in a civilized society. They held that it is morally wrong for anyone to take the material values their virtue had created and use it to serve values that were not their own.

What the self-reliant society did guarantee was that no one could stop you from producing wealth, and if you did produce wealth, you could use it to better your life. Whether you earned ten thousand dollars or ten million, you had the right to direct that money in the manner you believed would most improve your life. How much money you earned was fundamentally in your control. How much money you spent and saved was fundamentally in your control. As a result, your life was in your control.

This would have been the ethical way to continue dealing with the promise and the challenge of an industrial society. Americans should not have sought the chimera of a guaranteed income. Instead, they should have defined the principles individuals and societies must adhere to in order to make themselves progressively more prosperous and secure from life's challenges. Such an approach would have concluded that the keys are *self-reliance* and *economic freedom*, i.e., capitalism. Self-reliance leads people to rationally plan for their futures, given their unique goals, values, and resources. Economic freedom unleashes their work and creativity, allowing each person to maximize his production of wealth and achieve an ever more enjoyable and exciting life.

That is not the path we followed when we embraced the entitlement state. What we got was a raw deal. We gave up a limited government that respects property rights and economic freedom in exchange for less wealth, less progress, less opportunity, an entitlement crisis, and a morally troubled society.

Social Security and the entitlement state do not create wealth—they destroy it. If stealing means taking a person's property without his consent, then there is no fundamental difference between the entitlement state's lien on a person's income and the actions of a plain thief. The bureaucrat says "others" need the property more than the person who earned it. The thief agrees, declares that he is one of those "others," and proceeds to cut out the middleman.

Morally, the issue is not how *much* the government takes from you. The moral issue is: Does anyone have the *right* to take what you earn in order to give it to others—or does the product of your effort belong to you? A passage in Frederick Douglass's memoir, *Narrative of the Life of Frederick Douglass: An American Slave*, captures this perspective eloquently.

> I could see no reason why I should, at the end of each week, pour the reward of my toil into the purse of my master. When I carried to him my weekly wages, he would, after counting the money, look me in the face with a robber-like fierceness, and ask, "Is this all?" He was satisfied with nothing less than the last cent. He would, however, when I made him six dollars, sometimes give me six cents, to encourage me. It has the opposite effect. I regarded it as a sort of admission of my right to the whole. The fact that he gave me any part of my wages was proof, to my mind, that he believed me entitled to the whole of them. I always felt worse for having received any thing; for I feared that the giving me a few cents would ease his conscience, and make him feel himself to be a pretty honorable sort of robber.[200]

If confiscating all of a person's wealth is wrong, then how can seizing part of it be right? If stealing is wrong, then how can the entitlement state be classified as anything other than immoral?

Whose Life Is It?

The self-reliant society gave men unparalleled wealth, freedom, opportunity, and security. The entitlement state is at war with all that. It severely lowers our standard of living. And for what? We're told, for instance, that Social Security is necessary in order to prevent us from making short-sighted decisions, saving too little today to provide for our retirement needs tomorrow. Even most critics of Social Security concede that the goal of forcing people to save for old age is noble, even if Social Security does so in a less-than-perfect fashion. The truth is that even if Social Security were a government-enforced savings plan, it would severely reduce the control we have over our lives—and there is nothing far-sighted or noble about that.

Let me speak personally. I love my work and I plan on doing it until the day some unfortunate janitor finds me slumped over my laptop. I have no plans to retire and no desire to retire. Given my goals, I would choose to save enough to guard me against the financial risks of old age, but otherwise spend on my current priorities: everything from keeping my car running to saving for my daughter's education.

Contrast that with my dad. He's an avid golfer, and although he enjoys his job—he runs two different tech companies—he has always looked forward to a decade or two on the links and traveling the world with Mom. Given the choice, he would funnel as much money as he could into his retirement accounts.

And that's just the start. Even when it comes to saving for old age, we would almost certainly take different approaches. Our differing goals, knowledge, risk tolerances, time horizons—all of these would shape our respective choices.

There is not a one-size-fits-all life. Different people can rationally have very different goals and priorities, and if they are to live happy and successful lives, they have to be able to act on their judgment. The original American system recognized this fact, and so left individuals free to make their own choices. Social Security negates all that.

Social Security confiscates a huge portion of our wealth on the premise of "preparing us for old age." What you want from life, how you want to spend your money, how you want to spend your golden years—all of that is taken out of your hands. Your freedom to plan your own life? To hell with that. Your life belongs to politicians in Washington, and they will decide what's best for you. "If Social Security were voluntary," notes a revealing *Washington Post* article,

> it wouldn't be the rich who would opt out. . . . But many young people who find themselves hard-pressed to buy a home, educate children, or help aging parents might choose to avoid the relatively large slice that payroll taxes take from moderate wages. In time they—and their children—would come to regret that choice.[201]

There you have an open declaration that the entitlement statists want to control your life, because you are a child who cannot be trusted to plan your own affairs. Your job is to bow to the grownups in Washington.

The Gravest Injustice

But isn't it true that some people *would* make bad decisions if left free? Won't some people approach their retirement not simply differently but thoughtlessly and irrationally? Without a doubt. But what kind of a society punishes responsible people for the sake of the irresponsible?

This is the deepest evil of Social Security and the entitlement state: They punish virtue in order to reward vice. They do not stop people from being irrational and irresponsible. They just force the rational, the responsible, the *self-reliant* to pay the price. That is the essence of unfairness.

The grim joke is that this injustice makes people worse off—even those it claims to help. The world does not come divided into pre-determined castes of responsible individuals and irresponsible ones. There are some people who will consistently assume responsibility for their own lives no matter how rotten the society they live in. There are some who will default on responsibility no matter how virtuous their neighbors are. But the great majority of people are mixed. If they are surrounded by responsible men and if the incentives they face encourage responsibility, then they will tend to develop responsible characters. If they are surrounded by the opposite, they will tend to shrink in moral stature. The entitlement state makes the entitlement mentality the cultural default. It takes a significant amount of independence to rise above that default.

In a free society, reality, including the experiences of other people, acts as a man's teacher. In a society whose government does not pretend to guarantee people a retirement, anyone can know that the failure to plan leads to immense hardship and unpleasantness. If a person in such a society nevertheless chooses not to save, he—not those who make good choices—will suffer the consequences, which include a tighter budget or the discomfort that comes from asking his friends and family to bail him out. And he will remain free to do better in the future.

But in an entitlement society, where responsibility is discouraged, and where the reining morality denounces the self-reliant while praising the poor in spirit? We're seeing the results around us today. It is becoming easier and easier to shirk responsibility—and those who do shirk responsibility are assured that their course of action is both normal and moral. Imagine if some pushy school counselor pulled aside your child and said not to bother working hard, that success was just a matter of luck, and that he could always count on you to support him. That in effect is what the entitlement state has subjected all of us to. It is gut-wrenching to see so many people with so much potential choosing not to exercise it—to default on self-reliance because the culture they live in teaches them to think of themselves as helpless victims.

If some politician or intellectual believes that he knows what's best for others in old age, then let him privately try to persuade them to save and to invest more wisely. Let him even start a private, voluntary program modeled on Social Security if he wants. But by what right does anyone decide that he knows what's best for another adult and impose it on him by force?

Nothing good has come from Social Security. If we care about prosperity, choice, freedom, security, independence, or any other genuine value, then we should view FDR's "greatest achievement" as one of this country's worst failures.

CHAPTER SEVEN

Cashing In on Entitlement

W e've seen how Social Security punishes those who have to pay for it. We've seen how it sacrifices the rational and responsible Americans who would have otherwise tended successfully to their own affairs. We've even seen how it harms those genuinely unable to support themselves through no fault of their own—they too would benefit from living in a self-reliant society, in which those who *can* support themselves are best able to create the abundance on which the unable depend.

But there are two groups that Social Security and the entitlement state empower: those who seek unearned wealth, and those who seek political power. Ayn Rand elaborates:

> Morally and economically, the welfare state creates an ever accelerating downward pull. Morally, the chance to satisfy demands by force spreads the demands wider and wider, with less and less pretense at justification. Economically, the forced demands of one group create hardships for all others, thus producing an inextricable mixture of actual victims and plain parasites. Since need, not achievement, is held as the criterion of rewards, the government necessarily keeps sacrificing the more productive groups to the less productive, gradually chaining the top level of the economy, then the next level, then the next. (How else are unachieved rewards to be provided?)
>
> There are two kinds of *need* involved in this process: the need of the group making demands, which is openly proclaimed and serves as cover for another need, which is never mentioned—the need of the power-seekers, who require a group of dependent favor-recipients in order to rise to power. Altruism feeds the first need, statism feeds the second, Pragmatism blinds everyone—including victims and profiteers—not merely to the deadly nature of the process, but even to the fact that a process is going on.[202]

Far from all who receive benefits from the entitlement state are parasites. Most are part-victim, part-"beneficiary." They typically cling to the belief that they are receiving earned benefits, and would give them up if they really understood and faced the issue. But there are some bottom feeders who reap advantages they would never be able to obtain on a free market. These are the seekers of the unearned who couldn't care less where their money comes from—so long as it keeps coming without effort or moral reprobation. In a self-reliant society, the seekers of the unearned have to rely on begging, manipulation, or out-and-out crime to line their pockets. The entitlement state not only gives them virtually unlimited access to other people's wallets—it removes the stigma of being on the dole by allowing moochers to hide among the many decent people forced into the scheme. Worse, it morally elevates the moochers, who are transfigured into the vaunted "needy."

But they aren't "needy," not in any meaningful sense. Nor are they poor by historic standards. They live in squalor, but it is *self-made*. Theodore Dalrymple tells of the contrast between true poverty of the sort that enfolds India or Southeast Asia, and the so-called poverty of the moocher-filled communities created by the entitlement state (communities that, by Third World standards, are rich).

As a psychiatrist, Dalrymple would occasionally work with foreign doctors from the poorest parts of the world, who would marvel at the generosity of the British welfare state. "At the start they are uniformly enthusiastic about the care that we unsparingly and unhesitatingly give to everyone, regardless of economic status." Care that goes beyond medical assistance: "no one goes without food or clothing or shelter, or even entertainment. There seems to be a public agency to deal with every conceivable problem."

But that impression quickly begins to change as the visitors become familiar with some of the *recipients* of this generosity. Dalrymple recounts one doctor, originally from the Philippines, who wondered "why so few people seem grateful for what was done for them," a question sparked by an incident in which

> an addict who, having collapsed from an accidental overdose of heroin, was brought to our hospital. He required intensive care to revive him, with doctors and nurses treating him all night. His first words to the doctor when he suddenly regained consciousness were, "Get me a fucking roll-up" (a hand-rolled cigarette). His imperious rudeness didn't arise from mere confusion: he continued to treat

the staff as if they had kidnapped him and held him in the hospital against his will to perform experiments on him. "Get me the fuck out of here!" There was no acknowledgment of what had been done for him, let alone gratitude for it. If he considered that he had received any benefit from his stay, well, it was simply his due.

Over time, Dalrymple's guests would discover that this attitude was representative of the slum residents. "When every benefit received is a right, there is no place for good manners, let alone gratitude."[203] The observations would continue to pile up: neighborhoods filled with broken windows and piles of litter; public housing reeking of urine; people with no sense of responsibility or shame. Whereas the poor people of Africa or Asia generally lived with some dignity, many of the "poor" of the entitlement state were spiritually impoverished. "By the end of three months," writes Dalrymple,

> my doctors have, without exception, reversed their original opinion that the welfare state . . . represents the acme of civilization. On the contrary, they see it now as creating a miasma of subsidized apathy that blights the lives of its own supposed beneficiaries.[204]

But the worst, most immoral perpetrators are not the moochers who collect unearned rewards, but the entitlement statists who steer the system: the intellectuals, activists, and politicians who conceive, create, defend, and work to expand entitlement programs.

What the Entitlement Statists Want

What kind of society do the entitlement statists seek to create? What is their goal? Traditionally, their goals are put in terms of negatives. They are against poverty, inequality, injustice, capitalism. But what are they for? And what policies do they regard as achieving that goal? To these questions, you will get no clear answer.

But consider these two revealing facts: (1) The entitlement statists show virtually no concern for whether the entitlement state *actually* helps end poverty, and (2) they refuse to acknowledge or embrace the one proven means of achieving prosperity, free markets. Wealth redistribution is treated as inherently good and capitalism as inevitably bad.

In July 2013, Third World crusader and rock singer Bono made headlines when he said:

> Aid is just a stop-gap. Commerce [and] entrepreneurial capitalism takes more people out of poverty than aid. In dealing with poverty here and around the world, welfare and foreign aid are a Band-Aid. Free enterprise is a cure. Entrepreneurship is the most sure way of development.[205]

What made his comments so notable was that few anti-poverty crusaders acknowledge the most obvious fact about poverty: Capitalism cures it.

The fact that tens of millions of individuals in China and India have escaped dire poverty thanks to a somewhat looser economic leash elicits virtually no reaction from entitlement statists. What does? What animates them and gets their juices flowing? Only the prospect of creating new government programs, expanding government programs, curtailing capitalism, and raising taxes on the most productive members of society.

> If 75% of the wealth of the richest one-tenth of 1% of American society were immediately expropriated [rhapsodized left-wing philosopher Brian Leiter], there would be no need to discuss cuts to spending that affects the well-being of the vast majority. This is a democracy, why isn't this a major topic of public debate?[206]

President Obama, while not openly calling for confiscating large amounts of wealth, did push incessantly for raising taxes on high-income Americans. He called it a matter of fairness.

Taxing "the rich," Obama and other entitlement statists hold, is not a necessary evil. They do not say, "We regret that we have to increase taxes on successful Americans to help poor Americans." Instead, they sneer at and attack the very people they are counting on to foot the bill for their programs, the so-called rich. Obama went so far as to reject the idea that these victims earn their success, famously declaring to American businessmen that "You didn't build that." (Steve Jobs could not be reached for comment.)

Whenever you see people passionately crusading for a goal they refuse to name, you can be sure their goal is evil. The attack on successful Americans is not a misguided means to an end—it is the end.

What drives the entitlement statists—again, the leadership, not every person who supports entitlements—is hatred of the successful. What gets them out of bed in the morning is not a passion for the entitlement state, socialism, or any other system, but hatred of capitalism. They don't want poor people to be rich—they want rich people to be poor. Bono tells an anecdote that sums up this motivation:

> In Ireland people have an interesting attitude to success; they look down on it. In America, you look up at . . . the mansion on the hill and say, "One day . . . that could be me." In Ireland, they look up at the mansion on the hill and go, "One day I'm gonna get that bastard."[207]

This is the motivation of the schoolyard bully who pummels the straight-A student for making him feel inferior. It is the key to the entitlement statists' soul.[208]

The Egalitarians

There is no clearer admission of this soul than in the left's embrace of egalitarianism and its economic concomitant, economic equality. In a free society, economic inequality emerges from the fact that different people produce vastly different amounts of wealth. But, as Arthur Okun, chairman of Lyndon B. Johnson's Council of Economic Advisors, said:

> incomes that match productivity have no ethical appeal. Equality in the distribution of incomes . . . as well as in the distribution of rights would be my *ethical* preference. . . . To extend the domain of rights and give every citizen an equal share of the national income would give added recognition to the moral worth of every citizen.[209]

Offered a choice between a society where everyone is wealthy but some vastly wealthier than others, or a society in which everyone is equal but has less income than the poorest person in the unequal society, egalitarians prefer equal poverty over unequal prosperity. "Justice," writes one egalitarian philosopher, "requires the elimination of . . . inequalities, even if their elimination inhibits a further raising of the minimum."[210]

This is not a concern for helping lift people out of poverty. In fact, in the book that spawned LBJ's War on Poverty, socialist Michael Harrington admits that the poverty he had in mind was not absolute poverty—not the sort of poverty that sentences people to mud huts and starvation. He meant "relative poverty," i.e., being less rich than one's very rich neighbors.

> The American poor are not poor in Hong Kong. . . . They are dispossessed in terms of what the rest of the nation enjoys, in terms of what the society could provide if it had the will. . . . To have one bowl of rice in a society where all other people have half a bowl may well be a sign of achievement and intelligence. . . . To have five bowls of rice in a society where the majority have a decent, balanced diet is a tragedy.[211]

Is there real hardship in this country? There is—precisely to the extent that the government has stopped capitalism from working, reducing our opportunities to earn, keep, and invest wealth. But the entitlement statists never seek to reduce this hardship by *increasing* economic freedom, and instead keep endorsing policies to *decrease* economic freedom—even when such policies unambiguously harm struggling Americans. The only way to make sense of such a pattern is to recognize that reducing freedom is their goal.

You Are Not Your Grandfather's Keeper

What enables the entitlement statists to get away with it? How have they been able to fight for entitlement and against self-reliance while maintaining the moral high ground? By parading under the banner of "compassion," which, they say, consists of the belief that a person's *need* is a moral claim on achievement and that a person is "greedy" for wanting to keep what he earns—that a person has no right to exist for his own sake, but must serve and sacrifice for the needs of others. Recall the moral justification Bismarck offered for the entitlement state:

> [T]he modern state idea, the result of Christian ethics, according to which the state should discharge, besides the defensive duty of protecting existing rights, the positive duty of promoting the welfare of all its members, and especially those who are weak and in need of help, by means

of judicious institutions and the employment of those resources for the community which are at its disposal.[212]

This notion, that you are your brother's keeper, implies that the fact that you thought, planned, worked, and supported your own existence entitles you not to rewards but to the status of a servant. A servant of whom? Of anyone able to claim for himself the title of "weak and in need of help."[213] In her novel *Atlas Shrugged*, Ayn Rand unpacks the full meaning of this notion. To say that need is an entitlement, she argues, means that

> [I]t is immoral to live by your own effort, but moral to live by the effort of others—it is immoral to consume your own product, but moral to consume the products of others—it is immoral to earn, but moral to mooch—it is the parasites who are the moral justification for the existence of the producers, but the existence of the parasites is an end in itself—it is evil to profit by achievement, but good to profit by sacrifice—it is evil to create your own happiness, but good to enjoy it at the price of the blood of others.
>
> [This] code divides mankind into two castes and commands them to live by opposite rules: those who may desire anything and those who may desire nothing, the chosen and the damned, the riders and the carriers, the eaters and the eaten. What standard determines your caste? What passkey admits you to the moral elite? The passkey is *lack of value*.[214]

This is the philosophy and mentality behind the entitlement state. The entitlement statists' aim is not to eliminate poverty (which is one reason why they are so vociferous in fighting against any attempt to turn Social Security into a means-tested program: It would eviscerate their stronghold over most of the public). It's to eliminate those who eliminate poverty.

Traditionally, the entitlement statists have held the moral high ground. They do not deserve it. A system that sacrifices achievement to need is not a just system. A system that punishes virtue and rewards vice is not a moral system. A society that allows power-lusters to strangle the productive is not a compassionate society. The entitlement state is morally bankrupt.

CHAPTER EIGHT
The Nobility of Self-Reliance

It is not enough to make the case *against* Social Security and the ethic of entitlement. It is vital that we make the case *for* the virtues of capitalism and the ethic of self-reliance.

Self-reliance is the principle that each man is an independent, sovereign being, a fact which carries with it a profound responsibility if one wants to live: to support oneself through independent thought, productive effort, and voluntary cooperation with other sovereign men.

As a *thinker*, the self-reliant man takes responsibility for forming his own ideas and judgments. He doesn't just look around and do whatever everyone else is doing. He doesn't do whatever happens to feel good in the moment. He uses his best rational judgment and works to identify what will actually benefit his life over the long run. When it comes to his finances, for instance, he does not spend money today with no thought for tomorrow. He recognizes that he must plan for the future, including the possibilities of job loss, injury, and the challenges of old age.

The self-reliant man knows he is not immune from errors and mistakes, but he recognizes that the only thing more dangerous than submitting blindly to his own desires is submitting blindly to the desires and dictates of others. If others think he is making an error, he is open to being persuaded, but he does not recognize their right to force him to act against his judgment.

As a *producer*, the self-reliant man takes responsibility for paying his own way. He views productive work, not as a dreary duty, but as an avenue for prosperity, creativity, growth, fulfillment, pride, and joy. He does not wait for others to provide him with opportunities for success, and he does not envy the fact that others may achieve more than he does. His only concern is making the most of the opportunities he does have and of doing the best he is capable of. He refuses to be a victim of outside forces. He believes that success is fundamentally in his control, and he views any short-term failure as a chance to learn how to perform better in the future.

The self-reliant man does not desire the unearned. Although he loves money, he knows that a dollar earned by a man with self-respect is worth more than a fortune in the hands of a self-loathing parasite. He is not one of those walking inferiority complexes who lusts after riches so that he can impress those he envies and despises. His chief financial goal is independence—the ability to pursue the goals and values his mind desires. And because he earns what he gets, he does not feel guilty for his wealth. If he is poor, he is proud of the modest funds he does possess—if he is rich, he is proud of his fortune.

Just as the self-reliant man takes responsibility for thinking and producing, so he respects the right of others to think and produce in support of their own lives. He does not view them as a means to his ends anymore than he regards himself as a means to theirs. He deals with them, not by means of fraud, exploitation, manipulation, or coercion—but *trade*. "A trader," writes Rand,

> is a man who earns what he gets and does not give or take the undeserved. He does not treat men as masters or slaves, but as independent equals. He deals with men by means of a free, voluntary, unforced, uncoerced exchange—an exchange which benefits both parties by their own independent judgment. A trader does not expect to be paid for his defaults, only for his achievements. He does not switch to others the burden of his failures, and he does not mortgage his life into bondage to the failures of others.[215]

Together these traits formed the core of the early American character. It was self-reliance that enabled men and women to risk everything, traverse an ocean, and tame a continent. It was the fidelity to independent judgment that gave them the clarity and courage necessary to defy British rule and form the freest nation in history. It was a deep commitment to industriousness that made it possible for Americans to turn a virgin country into a land of plenty. It was a commitment to the trader principle that put an end to the notion that some men were a means to the ends of others.

These three principles—thought, production, and trade—have three political corollaries, which together made possible the original American system of government: individual liberty (the freedom to act on your independent judgment), the right to private property (the freedom to earn and use material wealth), and the principle of voluntary association (the freedom to deal with others as traders). The social system based on these three pillars is laissez-faire capitalism—the system in which the government exists only to protect individual rights, including private property rights. Under capitalism, the government's approach to the economy is: hands off.[216]

Capitalism, then, *is* the system of self-reliance. It is the system focused squarely on the individual. Society is not something above the individual to which he owes a duty. It is merely a group of individuals, each with his own dreams, goals, and purposes.

The entitlement statists attacked the self-reliant society at the root. They made three claims which add up to the conclusion that self-reliance is impossible and that an economic system based on self-reliance is therefore immoral:

1. Individuals are incapable of supporting their own lives and therefore require support from society.
2. Wealth is a social product and therefore society has a moral obligation to distribute it equitably.
3. A self-reliant society is a dog-eat-dog society in which only the strong survive and the weak go without help.

Find a Way or Make One

The entitlement statists deny that individuals are capable of running their own lives, arguing that men are too irrational or shortsighted.

Yet the fact is that the vast majority of Americans before the entitlement state *did* take responsibility for their own lives. Although their resources (and their educations) were often severely limited, they nevertheless demonstrated an admirable ability to make something of themselves. Success in a free country isn't an aberration—it is an achievement, and it's an achievement open to each individual's choice. Not every man can become Thomas Edison or Warren Buffett, but every man can succeed in running his own life.

Pick any disadvantage you'd like—poverty, ignorance, abuse, neglect, illness, discrimination, even total paralysis—someone has managed to blast through those obstacles and achieve success. Richie Parker, for instance, was born without arms but grew up to become a NASCAR engineer who designs (and drives) cars using only his feet.[217] An entitlement statist would chalk such successes up to dumb luck, but if you listen to the stories of those who succeed in the face of great obstacles, you inevitably find certain virtues at work. These are not people who sit around blaming others for their problems. These are not people who wait for someone to do them a favor. These are the men and women who live by Hannibal's great creed: "I shall find a way or make one."

One exemplar of this creed was John D. Rockefeller. When Rockefeller was sixteen he set out to find his first job. He made up a list of the companies he was interested in working for and then started knocking on doors, delivering a simple pitch: "I understand bookkeeping, and I'd like to get work." The first business Rockefeller approached turned him down. So did the second. But Rockefeller wasn't discouraged. For *six consecutive weeks* he spent six days a week going from business to business looking for a job and coming up empty. Once he had gone through his entire list, he simply started back from the beginning, visiting some companies two and even three times. Finally he was hired and won the chance to start his meteoric rise.

Another dramatic success story is that of Ben Carson. Carson, a black man, was raised in a poor household by a single mother whose own education ended in the third grade. Despite his inauspicious start, Carson decided at an early age that he wanted to become a doctor. He was not a naturally gifted student, however. Starting at the bottom of his class, Carson set an ambitious goal—to become the top student. He cut the amount of TV he watched, diligently studied, and used his free time to read widely. "Bennie," his mother told him, "if you can read, honey, you can learn just about anything you want to know. The doors of the world are open to people who can read."[218] Within two years Carson had achieved his goal—he was the top student in his class.

But his focus began to slip a few years later as he entered high school and started paying more attention to being "one of the guys" than earning high marks. When he realized that his grades had dropped, Carson revaluated his priorities. His mother had taught him, "I am the one ultimately responsible for my life." As he pondered his low grades he "began to realize that I had myself—and only myself—to blame. The in-group had no power over me unless I chose to give it to them."[219] He once again put his energy into his school work.

Eventually, thanks to his top grades and high SAT scores, Carson was able to attend college at Yale and later enter medical school at the University of Michigan. Once again he struggled, and once again he took responsibility for improving:

> During my second year . . . I got out of bed around 6:00
> a.m. and would go over and over the textbooks until I
> knew every concept and detail in them. . . . All during
> my second year, I did little else but study from the time I
> awakened until 11:00 at night. By the time my third year
> rolled around, when I could work on the wards, I knew my
> material cold.[220]

Shortly thereafter, Carson fell in love with neurosurgery, and chose it as his specialty. "*I have to know more*, I'd find myself thinking. Everything available in print on the subject became an article I had to read. Because of my intense concentration and my driving desire to know more, without intending to I began to outshine the interns."[221] He started taking over the responsibilities of the medical interns and residents, who would hand Carson their beepers and go nap in the lounge. Carson didn't mind—it gave him a chance to learn.

Ultimately, Carson's intense focus, ambition, and relentless commitment to learning would lead him to become a top neurosurgeon at Johns Hopkins. Reflecting on his path, Carson concluded:

> These young folks need to know that the way to escape
> their often dismal situations is contained within them-
> selves. They can't expect others to do it for them. Perhaps
> I can't do much, but I can provide one living example of
> someone who made it and who came from what we now
> call a disadvantaged background. Basically I'm no differ-
> ent than many of them.[222]

Rockefeller and Carson demonstrate the kind of tenacity that anyone can emulate and that will, in a free society, lead ultimately to success. (To the extent a society is not free, opportunity is limited and even eliminated, and success *does* become a matter of luck.) The entitlement statists will claim these are exceptions. That may very well be true, but what makes men like these exceptional is *not* that they succeeded despite great obstacles—it's that they chose to exercise the virtues success requires and achieved a *level* of success few have equaled. Success isn't easy *whatever* one's starting point, but it is within the reach of anyone willing to pay the price.

Just as each of us is capable of successfully earning a living, so we are competent to prepare for the future—including the possibilities of unemployment and illness, and the certainty of old age. We've seen, for instance, how self-reliant Americans built up savings, purchased insurance, and formed mutual aid societies to protect themselves. Today, the ability to prepare for life's challenges is far greater. We have much more wealth, many more tools, and a lot more knowledge and experience to draw on. All of the problems we've been told only the entitlement state can solve are in fact solvable through the voluntary decisions of free men.

You Did Build That

In President Obama's "you didn't build that" tirade, he perfectly captured the entitlement statist view of economics. The individual doesn't deserve his wealth or success, Obama said, because he doesn't create anything alone. Wealth is a social product and so morally it—or at least some undefined portion of it—belongs to society.

But wealth is not a social product. Wealth is created—it's created by, and morally belongs to, the individual creator. If Robinson Crusoe is tired of trying to scoop up fish with his hands and figures out how to turn a tree branch into a spear, increasing his daily catch tenfold, can Friday, who never thought to make a spear, properly complain that Crusoe has received an "unfair distribution" of fish?

Whatever the complications and intricacies involved, the basic issue is the same whether we're talking about a remote island or a complex division of labor economy like America's. An individual uses his mind and his existing property (i.e., previously created wealth) to bring new wealth into existence. On an island, his income consists of the wealth he produces. In a division of labor economy, his income consists of the value equivalent of the wealth he creates. In both cases, he is not taking wealth but making it.

Virgin's Richard Branson, for instance, got his start selling record albums out of the back of his car. The albums? They were his property. The money he made by selling them? His property. Branson used that money to implement his ideas for making records cheaper, phones more user-friendly, air travel more glamorous. He didn't grab a bigger piece of some socially produced pie any more than Crusoe did: He brought new wealth into existence.

Did Branson work with other people to create his products? Of course, but that doesn't change the essential issue. Each Virgin employee brought wealth into existence as an individual—and was paid accordingly. In a free market, there is an incentive not to pay a person more than his productive contribution, since no one wants to take a loss. But there is also an incentive to pay a person *in line* with his contribution, since competitors will be happy to snatch away an underpaid star.

What about the countless others who contribute *indirectly* to Branson's achievements? What about his parents? His teachers? Or the inventor of the airplane? The inventors of language? Obama's claim is that because these people don't receive financial remuneration for their contribution, Branson is profiting off their backs, and the government is there to make up for that sin with high taxes. Now, most of these people *were* paid for their services when they performed them. But even setting that aside, the fact that we receive benefits we don't have to pay for is not a failing of capitalism—it's one of its great achievements. What we actually owe such people is recognition and *gratitude* (which is more than the "you didn't build that" president offered them). The notion that we owe some undefined debt to "society," let alone to the government, is perverse. As Alex Epstein, founder of the Center for Industrial Progress, puts it:

> The fact that builders benefit from others in a free society does not mean that they should be forced to "give something back." It means we should all treasure living in a free society, and fight to make it freer. But if we are going to talk about who owes whom the most gratitude, then we should recognize that the biggest builders are owed the most. They have not only financed the lion's share of government, they have, more importantly, created the most enduring achievements. When I think of whom I owe gratitude to, it is individuals like Steve Jobs, not the millions of patrons of America's welfare state.[223]

Wealth is created by individuals, and in a market, absent government redistribution, that wealth rests in the hands of the individuals who created it. The "you didn't build that" argument is nothing more than an attempt to wipe out the distinction between those who earn money through productive work and those who take money from those who earn it.

Self-Reliance Is Not Dog-Eat-Dog

According to the entitlement statists, the self-reliant society is one in which the strong survive and the weak perish. If ever there was a view that was the complete opposite of the truth, this is it.

It was in the pre-capitalist world that the weak could not survive. During that era, men's existence was precarious and their opportunities for bettering their lives were virtually non-existent. Famine and plague would regularly wipe out the "surplus" population.

With capitalism came a population explosion. For the first time, the "surplus" population had a chance to survive. There was growing wealth, opportunity, technology, and knowledge. Food became more abundant and disease more scarce. For the first time in history, the so-called weak had a chance to survive and even prosper. As we've seen, anyone willing to take responsibility for his life can flourish under capitalism.

This is not to deny that responsible people sometimes struggle or encounter difficulties in a free society. Taking responsibility for your life doesn't automatically guarantee success—certainly not in the short run. You can make errors—costly errors—and accidents are always possible. But these are not shortcomings of freedom or black marks against self-reliance. They are inescapable facts of nature. It is disingenuous for entitlement statists to point to the fact that some children are orphaned or that some men become disabled or that some seniors mistakenly pour their savings into failed investments as proof that government intervention is the solution. Government has no magic wand to wave. It cannot solve these disasters—it can only create new disasters by restricting men's freedom. Its only ability is to force some people to pay for the mistakes and misfortunes of others. But that is an injustice, not a solution. The real solution is to leave men free to act on their own judgment and, if necessary, to seek voluntary help from others.

And in a self-reliant society, help is not hard to find. Self-reliance, remember, does not mean misanthropy. It doesn't mean moving to a shack in the woods and foregoing the benefits of dealing with other human beings. It means the commitment to live by one's own independent judgment and one's own productive effort, dealing with others in ways that are mutually beneficial.

Sometimes—though nowhere near as often as entitlement statists would have us believe—a person *committed* to paying his own way is unable to do so, through no fault of his own. When a man loses his job and accepts help from his friends and family while he searches for a new one, he has not defaulted on self-reliance. When a woman is struck with chronic back pain that keeps her in bed for months and accepts private charity to feed herself and her children, she has not defaulted on self-reliance. When an elderly couple has their life-savings stolen and moves back in with their children, they have not defaulted on self-reliance. Under such circumstances, self-reliance demands two things: that they get back on their feet as fast as possible, and that they show gratitude to those who have chosen to help them.

Gratitude comes from your recognition that it is no one's duty to help you—that their assistance is a product of their benevolence, their voluntary choice, and the value they place on you. It is true that some people help others out of a guilty sense of duty, on the premise that their moral obligation is to act as their brother's keeper. But this is far from the only reason to help others. It is not a selfless act of sacrifice to help those one loves. It is not necessarily a selfless act of sacrifice to give temporary aid to a friend or neighbor who is suffering through no fault of his own. It is not necessarily a selfless act of sacrifice to give to charity, if you think the cause is worthy and the cost is not a burden.

A self-reliant society is not a society where the tiny minority who are unable to support themselves are left on their own. It is a society in which one must appeal to the good will of others rather than hold out one's failure as a blank check on their time and resources. It is a society in which one must *ask* for help—not demand it at the point of a gun. We do not break into our neighbor's medicine cabinet claiming that our sickness entitles us to their drugs. The self-reliant society merely extends that same decency into the political realm, by denying people the ability to pursue their goals at the expense of other people's rights.

The entitlement statists would have us believe that, without wealth redistribution programs, deserving people would starve in the streets. Really? For someone in a free society to starve in the streets he would have to have no friends, no family, no extended family, no neighbors, no co-workers, no social clubs, no charities willing to feed him, and no capacity at all to take self-supporting action.

It is not the self-reliant society but the entitlement society that is callous and mean-spirited. It demands compassion for the bum who would rather collect a welfare check than work—and proceeds to finance that welfare check by taxing the young woman struggling to pay her way through college with a part-time job. The entitlement state gives government control over the schools—and proceeds to leave tens of millions of American children functionally illiterate. The entitlement state claims that Social Security is a moral imperative—but that a newly married couple's desire to spend their modest income on starting a family, rather than bankrolling someone else's retirement, isn't.

That is the true legacy of the entitlement statists. The entitlement state is not an ideal theory that produces some negative unintended consequences. It produces horrific consequences because its theory—that men are helpless tools of society—is immoral.

CHAPTER NINE

The Abolition of Entitlement

Social Security is immoral. Individuals thrive in a social system where they are free to pursue their own lives and happiness, dealing with others voluntarily. Social Security curtails individual responsibility, fleecing everyone, including the best individuals, for the sake of the worst. In a free society, people prosper to the greatest degree possible, and those who are unable to support themselves through no fault of their own can seek the help they need privately and voluntarily.

The evil of Social Security is a result, not of its details, but its essence. There is no moral way to violate individual rights, there is no moral way to dictate how a man spends the money he earns, there is no moral way to force people into a government retirement scheme against their will, there is no moral way to punish responsibility and reward irresponsibility.

Some critics of the entitlement state make a distinction between a government safety net and a redistributive state. They argue that redistributing wealth in the name of making people equal is immoral and destructive, but that a government safety net—a relatively small, means-tested minimum standard of living guaranteed by the government—is appropriate if not morally mandatory. Others oppose a government safety net in principle, but are willing to tolerate it on the grounds that it is more politically viable than the elimination of the entitlement state.

These are not tenable approaches. The same arguments and proposals were made by the critics of Social Security when it was first proposed. They, too, declared that individuals have an obligation to support those "in need," and that the government's job was to create a safety net to support them. Why did they fail? Because they were being inconsistent. Capitalism is based on the principle that your life and wealth belong to you. Once you concede that a person's need entitles him to others' wealth, then you necessarily concede the entitlement framework, which views self-reliance as immoral, and you open the door to anyone who can plausibly claim to have a "need" that is going unfulfilled.

The government safety-net view says that the government can draw a line somewhere between "real needs" and "unreal needs." But it can't. The entitlement statists will inevitably trot out examples of people who "need" something they don't yet have and declare that if we do in fact have an obligation to help those in need, then anyone who opposes entitlements for these people is revealing himself to be uncompassionate, cold-hearted, and immoral. Hence the relentless expansion of the entitlement state over the last seven-plus decades.

The only way to fight entitlements is to challenge the notion that a person's need is a moral claim on others, and to defend the principle that a person has a right to the wealth he earns through his own productive achievements. The only way to successfully fight entitlements is to show that they have *no* upside. They achieve nothing good and cause immense harm.

There is only one possible solution to a problem of this kind: Abolish Social Security and reestablish the self-reliant society.

Abolish Social Security? It seems unfathomable. But let's remember that America existed longer without Social Security than with it. Let's remember that a century ago, when Americans were far less wealthy than today, they were nonetheless able to deal with the challenges of preparing for old age on their own.

One reason that eliminating Social Security seems impossible is that we view eliminating it merely as *taking away* income from current recipients. We think of our mother, who is on a fixed income, and we wonder what would happen to her if she suddenly had $1,000 less each month.

But no sane plan to abolish Social Security would do so overnight. People at or near retirement not only may have planned their lives around the promise of Social Security, but thanks to the Social Security (and other entitlement) taxes they were forced to pay, their ability to save for old age was crippled. Any plan should make allowances for that. To advocate abolishing Social Security really means to advocate *phasing out* Social Security.

Keep in mind, the economic effect of eliminating Social Security will be to foster an incredible amount of productivity. Goods will become cheaper, more jobs will be available, innovation will increase—all of this will make the transition to freedom easier.

Let's not forget, though, that current and soon-to-be retirees will *have* to make do with fewer handouts. Members of these generations had an opportunity to fight against Social Security and for the American system. Most chose not to. They are more responsible for today's system than any other group, and it is wrong to make young people, who are not responsible for it, bear the principal burden.

What about "the promises society has made"? There is a wrong premise built into the question. It regards "society" as a collective agent that can make promises. But "society" is only a group of individuals: you, and me, and your parents, and your neighbor, and your mechanic, and Randy the bum, and Jasmine the hard-working attorney. Only individuals can make promises. I did not promise to pay for your Social Security. The "promise" of guaranteed retirement income supplied by unwilling victims, some below voting age, some not yet born, is not a promise *anyone* had the legitimate right to make. It is a "promise" that can be kept only by swindling the next generation. That is not a moral justification but a moral atrocity.

Similarly, phasing out Social Security would not deprive people of what they earned. Social Security is not a savings program, in which the money the government takes from you is saved and invested so that you can draw down on that investment in the future. Every penny taken from you today is immediately spent on current retirees (and other government functions). As Democratic Senator Robert Kerrey said in a 1998 Senate Finance Committee hearing, Social Security beneficiaries

> suffer under the illusion inflicted by us very often, that they have a little savings account back here [and] that they are just getting back what they paid in. They don't understand that it's just a transfer from people that are being taxed at 12.4 percent.[224]

Or, as another supporter memorably summed things up, Social Security is "a pipeline that goes from current workers to current beneficiaries."[225] The money taken from you in payroll taxes is spent. *That* is when you were deprived of what you earned and when you needed to fight against Social Security. The only way for you to get money now is for the government to raid the savings of your children, grandchildren, and other young workers—to tax *them* at 12.4 percent (or at a rate that is much, much higher). You cannot earn the right to seize from others what they have earned.

However, as vicious and as wrong as Social Security is, our goal should not be simply to end it. It should be to replace it with a positive: the original American system and the self-reliant society. We must not merely fight *against* entitlements—we must fight *for* the freedom, prosperity, and opportunity of the individual.

What would a new self-reliant America look like? It would be a world in which each individual would be responsible for his own life. He would be responsible for developing the knowledge and skills necessary to earn a living. He would be responsible for finding a job. He would be responsible for saving and planning for life's unexpected twists and turns, and for expected costs such as old age.

The vast majority of Americans would be up to that challenge, and would thrive thanks to the unparalleled expansion of freedom. Americans would prosper materially and spiritually, as they developed a sturdy foundation of self-esteem that comes from knowing that they are in control of their lives, their character, and their destiny.

Americans would feel a profound sense of optimism about the future. They would not have to fear government bureaucrats arbitrarily taking away their money or their pensions. They would not have to fear the devastating consequences of an entitlement crisis. They would not have to fear demagogues buying votes with their hard-earned dollars. They would not have to fear crippling interest rates brought on by inflation.

Social relationships in America would improve. We would start to see each other, not as moochers and milk cows, but as independent individuals who all get better together. We would live in a society of win/win, where everyone would have the greatest chance possible of making a better life for himself—not by reaching into others' pockets but by lifting himself up by his own bootstraps. It would be a society where no one would have to sacrifice for anyone.

We would also start to reestablish voluntary social institutions to help each other through tough times. We would learn to distinguish between parasites who want something for nothing and those who suffer through no fault of their own, and we would have more wealth than ever at our disposal, enabling us to help the people and causes we cared about. As for the parasites, we would be free to leave them to their own devices. Vice would be punished, virtue rewarded.

Life of course would still involve risks, and struggles, and hardships. Freedom does not eliminate life's challenges, but it does allow us to minimize life's negatives and maximize life's positives. It is the entitlement statists who have sold us the fantasy that if we just tax successful people enough, all such problems can be solved. They have promised us protection from nature in exchange for letting them rule men. A self-reliant America would offer us protection from other men so that we are free to face the challenges of nature.

That is what we should fight for, those of us who want to make the world a better place.

How to End Social Security

How do we best phase out and eliminate Social Security? That is the question economists, legal scholars, and policy experts should be thinking about. What we can say is that no plan will be without hardships. There is no clean way out of a messy situation, which is one more reason to avoid getting in messy situations.

How to end Social Security is not a particularly hard problem. The hardest problem is to get Americans to embrace the *goal* of eliminating Social Security. Once we do that, then the best minds should have no trouble finding a workable solution to get us there from here.

What principles should govern us in thinking about plans for the abolition of Social Security?

1. The plan should protect the rights of Americans to the greatest extent possible. This means, in part, that any plan should recognize the need to transition from Social Security (and other entitlements) over time.
2. No plan should give the government *new* powers to intervene in the market.
3. The ultimate goal must be total abolition—not a "better" means of forcing people to plan for retirement in a manner approved of by the state.
4. The plan should aim to move us from an entitlement society to a free society as quickly as possible.

There are many potential plans that would fit these criteria, but I want to address one common proposal that does not. The most popular policy advocated by critics of Social Security is Social Security "privatization." Although the details of these proposals differ, the basic idea is that the government should continue collecting Social Security taxes, but should place them into private accounts that individuals control.

Social Security privatization is based on the notion that the entitlement statists' ends are noble but their means are misguided—that it's right for the state to dictate how people plan for old age, but that it should force them into a scheme different from today's system. As we've seen, though, the very goal of Social Security is corrupt. An individual's life and wealth belong to him, and he has a right to decide how (or whether) to prepare for old age. A "privatized" Social Security would continue to allow government to decide what goals we set for our lives, and if we choose goals it does not approve of, to overrule our decisions. This is just as inconsistent with the self-reliant society as today's disaster.

But some Social Security privatization plans are worse than that. They wouldn't simply change today's system, they would introduce a new evil: They would give the government unprecedented new powers over the market. As Cato scholar Krzysztof M. Ostaszewski warns:

> Allowing the government to invest [Social Security dollars] in private capital markets would amount to the "socialization" of a large portion of the U.S. economy. The federal government would become the nation's largest shareholder, with a controlling interest in nearly every American company.[226]

Many critics of Social Security resort to privatization in the belief that it is an easier sell than abolition. This is not true. The same reasons that lead people to think Social Security is moral and necessary lead them to view markets and so-called market reforms skeptically. And if people are convinced that Social Security is a fundamentally destructive program, then they will want to see it eliminated, not "improved."

We don't need to privatize Social Security. We need to end it. Our goal must not be reform. It must be abolition.

A New Story of America

Is it too late? Have too many Americans become addicted to dependency to save this country? Thankfully, no.

Most Americans who receive entitlements do not think of the money as a handout. They have accepted the false notion that it represents income they earned through the taxes they have paid over the years. Yes, they believe that a person's need entitles him to handouts, but they bristle at the notion that *they* need a handout. A handout is what they see themselves as offering others. If they saw their entitlement check as a handout, they would not want it—or, at least, they would feel too ashamed to fight for it publicly.

Even many of those who do knowingly receive entitlement funds from the government are not fundamentally dependents. A common attitude is: "If I don't take it, someone else will." But if they had a choice between taking a handout or eliminating it for everyone (and paying less in taxes as a result), many would advocate eliminating handouts.

There surely are those who will fight any attempt to cut their entitlements. But the reason they have so much influence is not their sheer numbers, but the fact that they have been handed the moral high ground. If they had to openly state, "Yes, I want your money, money I didn't earn, and I should have it just because I say I need it," they would have no influence. They would convince no one and achieve nothing but their own ostracism.

Social Security and the entitlement state exist, not owing primarily to the financial desires of the recipients, but to the *ideas* of the public and its intellectual and political leaders. If those ideas are exposed as vicious, immoral, destructive, and anti-American, then there is every reason to expect that we will see a rapid change in American attitudes toward the entitlement state.

The entitlement statists won because of a culture-wide narrative that portrayed self-reliance as materialistic atomism, the pursuit of happiness as abject greed, the creation of unparalleled wealth as "zero sum," and the win/win society as a sewer of exploitation. The self-reliant society, the entitlement statists charged, impoverished the masses and obliterated the moral soul of America. It had to be reined in through a policy of massive wealth redistribution that would direct "society's" resources from "the greedy" to "the needy." The self-reliant society's unpardonable sin, they said, was to leave the individual "on his own."

There is a nugget of truth buried in this story. What made self-reliant America great *was* the fact that it was the first country in history where you were on your own. Understanding this fact provides the key to telling the *real* story of America.

Roll back the tape a few thousand years to when every element of life was controlled by the tribe. You could not live an independent existence, you could not choose your own ideas, your own values, your own destiny. You belonged to the group. The group, in turn, gave you a certain measure of protection: So long as you obeyed its commands, kept your place, and tended to its needs, you would get your scrap of food (if there was food to be had).

The story of freedom is the story of how the individual escaped from ownership by the tribe. As Ayn Rand once observed: "Civilization is the progress toward a society of privacy. The savage's whole existence is public, ruled by the laws of his tribe. Civilization is the process of setting man free from men."[227]

The Founding Fathers took a crucial leap forward in that process, declaring that the collective has no claim on you; that the government exists only to protect your right to live your own life, earn your own wealth, and seek your own happiness. Other people's wants and needs are not your responsibility.

The corollary was that you and you alone were responsible for securing your own wants and needs. You were responsible for developing the knowledge, skills, and traits of character you needed to earn a living. You were responsible for saving to meet life's unexpected twists and turns. You were responsible for educating your children. You could ask for help from other people—but you could not demand it as a right. You were on your own.

Did people shrink from the twin values of freedom and responsibility? On the contrary, the vast majority of Americans during the eighteenth and nineteenth centuries eagerly embraced life's challenges and flourished under the new system. People didn't flee from America, they fled to America. They came here poor, but ambitious—ready to carve out a life for themselves in a country that offered them the only thing they asked for: an open road.

Of course, Americans during this era were not "on their own" in the lone-wolf, asocial sense implied by the entitlement statists. As we've seen, free Americans developed complex webs of association based on voluntary agreement. An unprecedented division of labor—capitalists, businessmen, and workers coming together to create wealth on an industrial scale—was a product of this newfound freedom.

Far from leaving people unable to afford life's necessities, it was this system of voluntary cooperation that enabled the masses to afford modern luxuries—things like cars, microwaves, and air conditioning, which the wealthiest men of past eras did not own. What Americans of yesteryear lacked was not voluntary cooperation and trade, but involuntary servitude (slavery being the glaring, deplorable exception).

What did the entitlement statists' crusade to put an end to the "on your own" society consist of? They began replacing individual freedom, individual responsibility, and voluntary association with an entitlement society. They promised to keep the benefits of the industrial economy that capitalism had created, while replacing the freedom that had made it possible with a modern form of tribalism. The group would take responsibility for us from cradle to grave, and we in turn would become servants of the group, burdened with responsibility for the lives of others.

The Progressives and their present-day descendants have largely succeeded at eroding freedom. But the inevitable consequence is an economy nowhere near as vibrant as before. In a free country, you would decide how to live, whom to deal with, what obligations to accept, what projects to undertake, what values to uphold. But in entitlement America, you are forced to pay for other people's tonsillectomies, other people's Women's Studies degrees, other people's retirements, other people's business subsidies, other people's bailouts.

Yet it is the entitlement statists who have succeeded at damning self-reliance as immoral and have filled men with guilt for failing to adequately subordinate themselves to society. The question they have never answered is: Why? Why is man his brother's keeper? Why is it wrong for him to pursue his happiness, without exploiting others or allowing himself to be exploited? Why is it immoral for him to seek his own welfare, but moral for "the kept" to have their welfare served? Why does their happiness count, but his is sinful? Why on earth shouldn't a man seek to make the most of his own life, neither sacrificing himself to others nor others to himself?[228]

The entitlement statists' story of America is false. Self-reliance created no victims. It was, instead, the path to mutual success. The entitlement state is not compassionate. It is a moral and economic killer.

What We Must Do

Some critics of the entitlement state throw up their hands and say that it is too entrenched and that change of this magnitude cannot happen. But if *you* can be convinced, then any thinking person can be convinced, and that is all that's required to win. The question is not *can* we change people's ideas, but *how* can we change them?

This country has seen vast and rapid changes in thinking before:

from the propriety of breaking with Great Britain to our view of slavery, to women's suffrage, to gay marriage. In every case, the winning side triumphed by taking a principled stand in the name of the good. They *controlled the moral high ground*.

How do we take the moral high ground on this issue? This book, in essence, is my answer to that question. But let me make explicit some of the key takeaways.

If your position is right, then owning the moral high ground involves three basic tasks:

1. Make your conclusion—and your opponent's—fully clear.
2. Own all the positives.
3. Saddle your opponent with all the negatives.

One of the mistakes opponents of the entitlement state have made since the beginning is to "play defense." They have been against communism, and socialism, and Social Security, and Medicare, and welfare. But what have they been *for*? Aside from a few vagaries—"Americanism" for instance—there hasn't been an answer.

The result is that the entitlement statists are able to paint an inspiring (albeit false) picture of the future they want to create, and their critics are reduced to playing the role of the grouchy skeptic who bitterly pokes holes in their arguments and policies. "Your programs are expensive." "They won't work." "They lead to unintended consequences." All of that may be true. But you cannot win a debate if your position is that your opponent's vision is noble and yours is practical but immoral. If something is immoral then our top concern will be to minimize and eliminate it. If something is moral then our chief aim will be to find a way to make it work.

To seize the moral high ground, we have to offer our own *positive* vision, and finally put the entitlement statists on the defensive by explicitly naming their actual goals and conclusions.

What is our positive vision? We are for *capitalism* and the self-reliant society it produces.

We are for a system in which each individual is free to stand on his own feet, to work, to prosper, to carve out a life for himself—not one in which he must engage in a dog-eat-dog scramble to loot his neighbors, children, and grandchildren.

We are for a system in which each individual's right to life, liberty, property, and the pursuit of happiness is sacrosanct and where, as a result, all human relationships are *voluntary*.

In this debate, we must own every legitimate value at issue. *We* are for a society that nurtures freedom, justice, equality (before the law), opportunity, security, and prosperity, unlike our opponents who advocate a society that puts up roadblocks to achievement, sacrifices achievement to failure and irresponsibility, and caters to the hatred and envy of power-lusting politicians and intellectuals who have never achieved anything.

We must expose our opponents' claims to support self-reliance, capitalism, and Americanism. Saying Social Security promotes self-reliance is like saying castration promotes romance. Saying that capitalism is compatible with wealth redistribution is like saying that health is compatible with drinking arsenic. Saying that Americanism permits the entitlement state is a confession that one knows nothing about the founding of this country—and counts on the listener to know nothing too.

We must drop the platitude that our opponents' goals are noble, but their means are unworkable. Their goals are vicious and immoral. They want to turn us into servants of other people's need. If they truly wanted to enrich and empower individuals, they would not advocate a paternalistic program that impoverishes individuals.

Our opponents want to subvert the freedom, prosperity, independence, and community made possible by capitalism and the self-reliant society. Motivated by the same envy, insecurity, and lust for power that drives a schoolyard bully, they want to turn us all into dependents on the state. They want to callously exploit responsible, hardworking Americans in order to reward those who want something for nothing. Whatever their rhetoric, their chief goal is to destroy capitalism and self-reliance.

With that framework in mind, how do we criticize Social Security without ceding the moral high ground? The primary criticism of Social Security should not be that it is unsustainable. That implies that it *should* be sustained, but unfortunately *can't* be. We must go deeper and show that Social Security *shouldn't* be sustained because it subverts self-reliance and everything self-reliance requires and implies.

Finally, we must learn to openly acknowledge challenges that people face under freedom without conceding the moral framework of our opponents. Freedom is a necessary requirement of human flourishing, but not a sufficient one. It is an inescapable fact of nature: Everything we value has to be earned by our own thought, choice, and effort. If we don't take responsibility for our own life, then no political system can change the fact that we will not achieve success and happiness.

Even if we do take responsibility for our own life, nothing *guarantees* success. We must continually learn how to cope with life's challenges. How, for instance, should free men deal with the risk of unemployment? Through individual savings? Mutual aid? Insurance? Some other approach that has yet to be imagined? Freedom doesn't provide an automatic answer—but it does allow each of us to search for the best answer.

The key point we must make is that freedom doesn't *create* challenges—it is the political condition that gives us the greatest ability to deal with *nature's* challenges. Although freedom doesn't guarantee we will meet those challenges successfully, restricting freedom does guarantee we will fail.

These are the key principles with which we can take the moral high ground and change the way people think about Social Security.

Some say that it is too late to win the war of ideas and we must focus on winning elections. The truth is that it's too late to focus on winning elections. The right has won elections. Look at what we got in return: Republican presidents have increased government spending even more than have Democrats. Nothing is more impractical than starting at the level of practical politics. So long as Americans support entitlements, you will not find any political support for getting rid of them. Nor can we expect a candidate for public office to lead the educational campaign. An election primarily involves appealing to existing constituencies—not persuading people to adopt new ideas. A political campaign is not an educational enterprise.

Some say that holding a radical position—the complete abolition of Social Security and entitlements, generally—is a handicap and we should try to hide or soften our goal. But the truth is that *only* a consistent opponent of entitlements can control the moral high ground. Compromisers and appeasers may offend fewer people in the short term, but in the long term they cannot stop the march of the entitlement state—and they often work to accelerate it. The compromisers may have a seat at the table, but that seat has bought them nothing in terms of reining in Social Security or other entitlements. Principled opponents of entitlements may be frozen out of the debate today, but once we earn our seat at the table, it will be the entitlement statists who are on the defensive and eager to compromise in *our* direction.

There are no two ways about it. We must fight a war of ideas. But to win the war of ideas, we will have to "up our game" by an order of magnitude. Those of us who oppose the entitlement state must get better at telling the story of how Social Security is harming America. We must learn to move hearts and minds, and to form a consistent, uncompromising case against Social Security. We must write better, speak more eloquently, be more ruthless in our commitment to truth and accuracy. We must take on the hardest objections and provide the most persuasive answers. We must think deeply about *why* people reject our views and have not been persuaded by our efforts so far, and then we must improve, continually and continuously. I'm reminded of a quote from economist Henry Hazlitt that I keep on my office door:

> A minority is in a very awkward position. The individuals in it can't afford to be just as good as the individuals in the majority. If they hope to convert the majority they have to be much better; and the smaller the minority, the better they have to be. They have to think better. They have to know more. They have to write better. They have to have better controversial manners. Above all, they have to have far more courage. And they have to be infinitely patient.[229]

What You Can Do

Do you want to help create a self-reliant society, where each individual is free to make something of his own life? This is the cause of our time, and there is no greater crusade to join.

What can you do? First and foremost: Know your case and then speak out. A new culture of self-reliance is possible, but it is the product of many individuals *living* self-reliantly and self-confidently *championing* self-reliance. Whether it is in a quiet conversation with a friend or a Facebook post or an op-ed in the *New York Times*, public opinion is made by those who choose to make their case, on whatever scale is open to them.

The simplest and probably most effective way to speak out is to help promote the work of the best free-market intellectuals. Distribute their work on social media. Send it to Congressmen, businessmen, or any influential leader you think might be open to it. Hand it to friends and family. Plaster it on billboards. Socialism came to dominate Europe through this method, and we can use it to our advantage today.

A more ambitious but incredibly powerful way to get your message out is to form groups and organizations to be advocates for self-reliance and against Social Security. There are already groups that provide an alternative to AARP—all the great discounts, none of the lobbying for the entitlement state. There are even groups modeled after mutual aid societies. One group that does not exist but should is a lobbying organization on the order of "Social Security Recipients Against Social Security," which would establish a base of support for political candidates who want to rein in the system. And young Americans, the biggest victims of the entitlement state, should form equivalent organizations.

Whatever you choose to do, on whatever scale you choose to do it, though, the key is to speak. If you want to fight for a better world, tell your story. Explain to people that you know self-reliance is possible—because *you* have achieved it in your own life. Inspire others with your success story. Tell them what obstacles you had to overcome, tell them what barriers you had to blast through in order to get from where you started to where you are now. Acknowledge all of those who helped you along the way, but do not fail to explain that none of that help would have made a difference had you not sought it out and made use of it through your own initiative and effort.

Tell people that self-reliance is *rewarding*. Explain the difference between being able to take pride in your work and gobbling up the unearned like a stockyard animal. Help them see that a million dollars will not buy happiness for a man who cannot look himself in the mirror each morning. Let them know what it is like to be a *man*—who lives on his own terms and earns people's genuine respect, not their pity, fear, or envy.

Speak out for individual responsibility. Self-confidently tell the world that "Your retirement is not my problem." You have a right to live for your own happiness, to spend your resources on yourself and the people *you* care about. Be unapologetic in declaring that no one has a right to a single dime you've earned—and that, although you may help others, you do so on your terms, by your own choice, and that you will never lift so much as a finger to help someone who declares that he has a *right* to your aid.

Above all, when you do speak of political policies, remember that *you* hold the moral high ground. Don't adopt a defensive posture. Don't seek to prove that you care about those who suffer through no fault of their own—that should not be treated as a matter open to question. Don't try to hide, soften, or apologize for wanting to abolish the entitlement state—follow the original abolitionists who refused to apologize for wanting to wipe out an evil institution in order to expand individual freedom. *That*, and nothing less, is what it takes to change the world and to resurrect the American way of life.

Finally, there is one thing that you need *not* do if you want to fight against Social Security: You do not need to refuse Social Security benefits. On the contrary, it is only *opponents* of the entitlement state who have a moral right to accept entitlement payments—so long as they regard it as restitution and are prepared to give them up in exchange for freedom. As Ayn Rand explains:

> Since there is no such thing as the right of some men to vote away the rights of others, and no such thing as the right of the government to seize the property of some men for the unearned benefit of others—the advocates and supporters of the welfare state are morally guilty of robbing their opponents, and the fact that the robbery is legalized makes it morally worse, not better. The victims do not have to add self-inflicted martyrdom to the injury done to them by others; they do not have to let the looters profit doubly, by letting them distribute the money exclusively to the parasites who clamored for it. Whenever the welfare-state laws offer them some small restitution, *the victims should take it.*[230]

To accept such payments does not make one a hypocrite. The key is not to place any short-term financial consideration above your commitment to abolishing the entitlement state and establishing a free, self-reliant America. That is the goal we must fight for and never surrender.

What are our chances of success? And on what time scale? I have no idea, and frankly I think it's a pointless question. If you know that a course of action is right and there is a chance you can win, then you fight, regardless of the odds and regardless of how long it will take. The alternative is to lie down and die.

And what we do know is, there is a chance. So long as we have free speech, we can make a rational case and men are free to listen to reason. We still have that freedom. Let's use it.

APPENDIX
End the Debt Draft

Forty thousand dollars. That's roughly your share of the U.S. national debt. That's bad, but it's nothing compared to the debt the government's going to be racking up in the years ahead thanks mainly to America's old-age welfare programs.

As the Baby Boomers retire, the bill for Social Security and Medicare will grow fast, setting off a debt tsunami. Economists can estimate the difference between how much government is on track to spend and how much it will raise from taxes. They call this "the fiscal gap." That number is astronomical: $205 trillion dollars, or more than half a million dollars per person.[231]

Today, you and millions of other young Americans are being *drafted* into debt. Like the military draft, the Debt Draft treats the lives of young people as the property of the state. You have been conscripted to finance other people's retirement and health care needs, regardless of what impact this will have on your life. Your duty is to set aside your own happiness in order to serve the needs of the old.

Responsible individuals only take on debt they can manage, and only when it serves important goals and values: to go to college, buy a home, start a business. But imagine being forced to pay someone *else's* student loan debt, or someone *else's* mortgage, or someone *else's* credit card bill. Would that be fair? Of course not. But that is what the Debt Draft amounts to.

Now, let me be clear. Whatever the parallels between today's debt disaster and the military draft, there is a vast difference. The military draft left countless young Americans maimed or killed, which is something that we should be careful not to trivialize. But there *is* a parallel between that and the welfare state that we must not ignore. Both turn young people into servants.

The welfare state has always involved transferring wealth from the young to the old. Each generation was told, in effect: "Your parents' and grandparents' generation will exploit you today, but don't worry—someday you'll get to exploit your children's and grandchildren's generation for a whole lot more than you ever paid in taxes." The difference is that the bill you'll be handed is so large that its effects can no longer be ignored: Unless we do something, it is going to rob you of many of your hopes and dreams.

The math is straightforward. Right now, the average elderly American receives $30,000 from the welfare state annually, with that number expected to rise to $40,000 two decades from now. Meanwhile, there will be fewer workers to carry that burden. When the welfare state was first created, there were forty workers to support each recipient. Today there are only three. As the Baby Boomers continue to retire, that number will drop to around two. That means you'll be responsible for $20,000 a year to support your elders, in *addition* to whatever other taxes you'll have to pay to support the government's other functions. That's the equivalent of buying someone else a new car each year—and, of course, we haven't even mentioned state and local taxes.[232]

But let's be clear: The Debt Draft isn't a problem tomorrow—it's a problem right now. The average college graduate starts out making about $45,000 a year. Well, you have to hand over 15.3 percent of that—$6,750—to current retirees just to fund Social Security and Medicare Part A. That's not a new car a year, but it's more than enough to make monthly payments on a new car. Is it any wonder that young people are waiting longer to move out of their parents' house, waiting longer to start families, and are saving next to nothing?

That's the bad news. Here is the good news. A solution *is* possible— one that will not only ward off catastrophe, but one that will make America a freer, more prosperous, more *moral* nation. But we have to act soon.

Why You're Being Exploited

Parents don't generally steal from their children. On the contrary, they work hard to make sure their children will have a better life. So how did we get to where we are today?

America didn't always have a welfare state. It is actually a relatively recent phenomenon. For the first 150 years this country existed, each person was responsible for supporting his own life through productive work (slavery being a deplorable exception). The government didn't redistribute wealth. It didn't take one person's property and give it to others. As Jefferson warned, "To take from one . . . in order to spare others . . . is to violate arbitrarily the first principle of association, —the guarantee to every one of a free exercise of his industry, & the fruits acquired by it."[233] Instead, the government protected each person's right to work, to keep what he earned, and to use it to build a life for himself.

With government's functions limited, its costs were low. With the exception of the Civil War, federal government spending during this nation's first 150 years hovered around 3 percent of GDP (today it is more than 20 percent). Before the welfare state was created in 1935, federal debt never hit 40 percent of GDP, even in wartime, and often stayed below 10 percent (today our debt is closing in on 100 percent of GDP).[234]

It was during this era that America became the mightiest economy in history.

The Collectivist Revolt

Not everyone approved of this individualist system—most notably the leading intellectuals of the late nineteenth and early twentieth centuries. They called themselves "Progressives" for the reason that they believed America needed to "progress" beyond the principles of the Founding Fathers. They rejected the principles of limited government. They wanted a government with expansive powers that could be wielded for what they considered the "national interest."

"You know that it was Jefferson," recalled leading Progressive Woodrow Wilson, "who said that the best government is that which does as little governing as possible. . . . But that time is passed." Instead of a limited government, he wrote elsewhere, "Government does now whatever experience permits or the times demand."[235]

The Progressives were *collectivists*. Their theories amounted to the view that, in philosopher Ayn Rand's words, "the individual has no rights, that his life and work belong to the group . . . and that the group may sacrifice him at its own whim to its own interests."[236] They did not approve of the American system, which enshrined individual freedom and individual responsibility. According to Herbert Croly, another leading Progressive, Americans needed to forswear their own happiness and devote themselves to "individual subordination and self-denial" for the sake of the collective. "[T]his necessity of subordinating the satisfaction of individual desires to the fulfillment of a national purpose," he added, "is attached particularly to the absorbing occupation of the

American people, —the occupation, viz.: of accumulating wealth."[237]

When it came to the economy, then, a major part of the Progressive platform was the creation of an American welfare state. Welfare programs would transfer wealth from those who earned it to those who didn't but allegedly needed it. Whatever the source of a person's need—whether it was bad luck or bad choices or his own immorality—the sheer fact that he needed something would mean that others had a duty to serve him. Individuals would no longer be able to focus on making the most of their own lives. They would have to set their own hopes and dreams aside and spend a substantial part of their lives working to take care of the needs of others.

Social Security and Medicare

For nearly half a century, Americans rejected Progressive demands for a welfare state. The first major welfare program didn't come until 1935. The Social Security Act was signed into law by Franklin Delano Roosevelt, who shared the basic philosophy of the Progressives but preferred to speak of "improving" or "updating" America's founding principles rather than rejecting them.

Social Security was a government retirement scheme in which the government would tax current workers in order to pay for retirement benefits for the elderly (generally those 65 or older). The program would grow from a relatively small part of the government's budget to the most expensive program in American history. Today Social Security takes more than $700 *billion* from workers each year and hands it out to retirees.

From the start, the Progressives also advocated a welfare program to cover health care. FDR sympathized with this goal, but the political opposition to a government takeover of health care was too intense in 1935. It would take another thirty years before Lyndon B. Johnson signed Medicare into law.

The details of Medicare are complex, but the basic idea is simple. Just as Social Security taxes younger Americans in order to provide retirement benefits to the old, so Medicare taxes younger Americans in order to provide health insurance benefits to the old.

When it came to the costs of Medicare, they went out of control almost immediately. Like Social Security, the program faced the problem of fewer workers supporting more and more beneficiaries.

But it also encountered another problem: When people were offered virtually free health care, their demand for it turned out to be virtually unlimited. Shortly after Medicare was created in 1965, Americans were told it would cost $12 billion by 1990—its actual cost was $98 billion. Today Medicare costs working Americans $600 *billion* a year—and that number is projected to nearly *double* over the next decade, reaching $1.1 trillion in 2023.[238]

Welfare State Exploitation

That's where we are today. Remember that working Americans already pay 15.3 percent of our income to fund Social Security and Medicare—more than $6,000 a year for many of us. And, of course, those taxes will have to increase substantially to keep the system going in future years.[239]

Think of what this does to young people who are just trying to start out in life. Six thousand dollars a year—to say nothing of $20,000—can sentence a person to a high-crime neighborhood, keep him from starting a family, or force him to stay at a dead-end job rather than following his dream to start a business.

The question we need to ask is: *Why?* Why did we create this system and why do so many people continue to support it? Is there any reason to support it? What could possibly justify exploiting America's youth?

The conventional answer consists of five myths: (1) the Earned Benefit Myth, (2) the Generational Pact Myth, (3) the Poverty Myth, (4) the Security Myth, and (5) the Compassion Myth.

The Earned Benefit Myth

Myth: Young people are not being exploited. Older Americans earned their benefits by paying in to the system during their working years.

Fact: First of all, we need to realize that Baby Boomers are scheduled to receive about $300,000 more from the government than they ever paid in taxes. (Meanwhile, your future children are slated to *pay* about $400,000 more in taxes than they will ever receive from the government.)[240]

More important, the money taken from the Baby Boomers when they were young was not saved and invested to provide for their future. If it had been, there wouldn't be a debt crisis. Instead, every penny taken from them was immediately spent by the government. The only way for them to get their "earned benefit" is to take money from you and your children.

It's true that some older Americans are dependent on Social Security and Medicare: A lot of the money they could have used to prepare for old age was taxed away to support *their* parents and grandparents. But that doesn't make their Social Security check an earned benefit. You cannot earn the right to exploit people—even if you were once the victim of exploitation. You don't have the right to rob people just because you were once robbed.

Social Security and Medicare do not deliver earned benefits. They are welfare programs, plain and simple.

The Generational Pact Myth

Myth: Old-age welfare programs represent a pact between generations: our promise to take care of those who once took care of us.

Fact: There can be no such thing as a "pact" consisting of one generation's determination to loot future generations.

Parents don't breed servants—they create sovereign individuals. Children don't choose to be born, and so while parents have an obligation to support their children, children have no moral obligation to support their parents. They might choose to do so out of goodwill, but their parents cannot *demand* it as a matter of right.

What's true at the individual level goes doubly for society as a whole. If we don't owe support to our own parents, we certainly don't owe it to strangers we have never met.

In an individualist society, each person is responsible for his own life, including his own retirement and his own medical needs. If an elderly American needs help, he is free to seek others' voluntary assistance. If a young American wants to provide help, he is free to do so. But no one is born into this world beholden to others.

The Poverty Myth

Myth: Without Social Security and Medicare, millions more Americans would be in poverty.

Fact: The path to prosperity is not welfare state looting but the free market. Had we continued to follow individualist principles, most Americans today would be far richer.

Before we examine the effect of welfare programs on the economy, however, we need to step back and look at the big picture. Poverty is mankind's natural state. In the era before capitalism emerged during the early nineteenth century, even citizens of relatively prosperous nations lived on only a few dollars a day. The free market created by the individualist society gave individuals the greatest possible freedom and incentive to produce. Anyone with an idea for how to do things better was free to give it a try. And if he succeeded? The rewards were his to enjoy. The result was an outpouring of ability and ingenuity on a scale the world had never seen.

It was an era in which people's incomes quadrupled, life expectancy climbed from under forty to over sixty, and science and technology revolutionized the way we lived. Millions of immigrants flooded into the country, seeking to make a life for themselves in "the land of opportunity."

Life, to be sure, was still hard. It had *always* been hard. But it was better than it had ever been and it was improving faster than it ever had, as free individuals lifted themselves out of poverty and into prosperity.

It was when welfare state spending really took off during the late 1960s that America's poverty rate *stopped* declining.[241] This shouldn't come as a surprise. When the welfare state transfers money away from the people who create it, it undermines how much wealth gets produced in the first place.

If the individualist society provided people with the greatest possible freedom and incentive to produce, then the welfare state curtails that freedom and dampens those incentives by taxing work and subsidizing idleness and dependency. Social Security, for instance, incentivizes enormously productive workers—workers with decades of knowledge and experience—to stop working years before they might otherwise retire. (If you continue working and earning money after you apply for early benefits, your benefits are reduced.)

At the same time, a substantial portion of the wealth doled out by the welfare state is taken out of the hands of people who would have saved and invested it, and put into the hands of people who consume it, while also making people feel as if they have no *need* to save. This has contributed to the collapse of America's national savings rate from around 15 percent to just about *zero*.[242]

This is a disaster: It is savings and investment that increase our standard of living over time. The less we save and invest in things such as more efficient factories, better machinery, and research and development, the less technological innovation, productivity, and prosperity we'll see. That's how we raise our standard of living. As individuals produce more, they earn more—and the more they earn and save, the more they can produce in the future. Rising productivity is the cure for poverty and the path to prosperity.

The welfare state did not end poverty—it reduced prosperity. The result, for the average American, has been to make our income far lower than it would have been had we never embraced the welfare state. By how much? It's impossible to say precisely. But consider this: If, starting in 1870, economic growth had been just 1 percent lower each year than it was, our standard of living today would be lower than Mexico's. One economist estimates that the welfare state has lowered the income of the average American by 25 percent *before he pays a single penny in taxes*.[243]

It is in this context that we have to evaluate the fact that poverty among the elderly has declined significantly since Social Security was created. There is every reason to suspect that if Americans had been free to keep and invest their money, poverty among the elderly as well as other groups would have declined even faster.

In any case, we cannot ignore the *victims* of Social Security. To the extent Social Security made older Americans better off, it did so by making younger Americans *worse* off. In America before the welfare state, one person's prosperity didn't come at anyone else's expense—his gains made others *better* off. Contrary to what we've been taught, it's not capitalism that is dog-eat-dog: It's the welfare state.

You might wonder at this point: If the welfare state is so economically destructive, then how is it that America has become richer in the years since Social Security? The short answer is that we have grown richer *despite* welfare programs, not because of them.

If welfare state programs were the cause of our prosperity, then it is curious that economic progress started more than a century before the welfare state was created and has *slowed*, not sped up, in recent decades. If welfare programs were the cause of our prosperity, then Western Europe—which has a much more expansive welfare state—should be the most prosperous place on the planet. Instead, countries such as Greece, Spain, and Italy are in crisis, with France doing only marginally better. And several countries, such as Sweden, have found that after reining in their welfare state programs, their economies have gone from moribund to robust.

If you care about prosperity, your first priority should be resurrecting America's free market. If you support the welfare state, you've given up any right to claim that you care about improving Americans' standard of living.

The Security Myth

Myth: The individualist system creates immense economic insecurity among the elderly, who often cannot work and yet don't have enough money to retire or to pay for needed medical care. Only a welfare state can provide a safety net to relieve this insecurity.

Fact: Creating a system in which other people can take your wealth whenever they decide they "need" it is the antithesis of security. True security means that you, your freedom, and your property are sacrosanct.

The free market not only provides that security and maximizes your ability to prosper in your younger years—it enables you to use your resources to prepare for old age and create a robust *private* safety net.

For starters, you can diversify your investments or purchase annuities (in essence, guaranteed streams of income). You can purchase various forms of insurance. And not only familiar forms of insurance, such as health or life insurance. In America before the welfare state, individuals often insured themselves against economic risks including permanent disability and job loss.

As for health insurance, a free market provides ample ability for you to insure against old-age medical costs. In fact, before Medicare, most elderly people were able to get the health care they needed. A *growing* number (more than half by 1960) carried insurance, while the others paid out of pocket, relied on friends and family, or turned to private charity. (It's worth noting that even with Medicare, today's seniors are paying about the same amount out of pocket for medical services as they were *before* Medicare, and that their coverage does not even provide catastrophic protection: Hospitalized for over 150 days? Medicare doesn't cover that. Need long-term care, such as a nursing home? Medicare doesn't cover that.)[244]

There were certain challenges faced by the elderly when it came to getting health insurance. But these problems were created by the government. In particular, the government gives huge tax preferences to health insurance purchased through one's employer, and by the 1960s, many Americans were covered under employer-sponsored plans. The trouble was that many Americans eventually retired. At a time when their health risks were highest, these Americans found themselves having to purchase new health plans at rates far above what they had been paying. Absent this tax preference, few people would have elected to get insurance through their employer. Instead, they could have entered into long-term contracts directly with insurers to guarantee that they would have affordable coverage when they reached old age.

Finally, in a free market you can seek support from your friends and family if you need it. You may choose to spend your final years living with your children and grandchildren. Or if you want to remain independent or don't want to impose on your family, you are free to accept their financial support.

What would happen to very poor elderly Americans in an individualist society in cases where they have no friends, family, or neighbors they can turn to for help? They can ask for private charity, which has always been abundant in America. "In fact," writes historian Walter Trattner of the era before the welfare state, "so rapidly did private agencies multiply that before long America's larger cities had what to many people was an embarrassing number of them. Charity directories took as many as a hundred pages to list and describe the numerous voluntary agencies that sought to alleviate misery, and combat every imaginable emergency."[245]

How effective are these strategies? If we look at history we find that the elderly did so well that, as late as World War I, even those pushing for an American welfare state did not argue that old age was a major source of poverty and insecurity in the United States.[246] That's incredible when you recall that capitalism had only started to remedy pre-industrial poverty, and that America was welcoming about a million immigrants a year, many of them poor, uneducated, and unskilled.

The welfare state, by contrast, makes old age *more* precarious. It saps us of resources when we are young and healthy and leaves us largely at the mercy of the government: Our income consists of whatever politicians decide to give us at the moment. The Debt Draft isn't making us more secure—it's impoverishing us and may one day push the greatest nation in history off the edge of a financial cliff.

The Compassion Myth

Myth: The individualist system is immoral. It demonstrates a cruel lack of compassion for those who hit hard times and are unable to support themselves. Old-age welfare programs represent society's compassion for some of its most vulnerable citizens.

Fact: A moral society is one which above all respects the *rights* of individuals—their right to make something of their lives and to dedicate their days and hours to the pursuit of their own happiness. It's a society in which each of us is responsible for our own life, and we deal with others only on the basis of their *voluntary* consent. It is, in other words, a society based on the principle of individualism, not collectivism.

If you want to get a college education, a moral society is one in which you and your parents have to set aside income or find someone willing to give you a loan—you are not entitled to a subsidy at my expense. If a retiree wants the latest arthritis treatment, a moral society is one in which he has to pay for it or ask others to help him—he isn't entitled to raid your savings account.

This does not represent a regrettable burden, but a great privilege. In a moral society, we get to decide what we want out of life and pursue it as we see fit—we aren't forced into a one-size-fits-all retirement or medical program. Our only limitation is our ambition and ability.

But under the welfare state, you have no right to a single penny you earn if someone else "needs" it more. Your parents, for instance, might have worked sixty-hour weeks for twenty years in order to afford to pay for your education. But a welfare state has no compunction about seizing your college fund and giving it to elderly citizens if it decides their "need" outweighs yours.

When need is viewed as a moral entitlement to other people's money, time, and effort, you get the worst injustice imaginable. People are punished for their success and rewarded for their failure. The more ambitious and self-responsible a person is, the more he owes to others. The more lazy and irresponsible he is, the more others owe to him. As for the tiny few who are truly helpless through no fault of their own, they are trotted out by welfare statists in order to disguise and whitewash this injustice.

Looting innocent victims is not compassionate but immoral. It's immoral when rich people plunder poor people—and it's immoral when poor people plunder rich people. It's immoral when the powerful minority exploits the majority—and it's immoral when the majority helps itself to the property of the minority. It's immoral when young people mooch off the old—and it's immoral when old people mooch off the young. If the essence of justice is that each person receives his due, then it is only a society that protects the rights of *every* citizen that can be called a just, fair, or *human* society.

The desire to show compassion is not a moral blank check that can justify treating other people as a means to your supposedly noble ends. If you want to help your grandfather or someone else's grandfather pay his bills, then in an individualist society, you're free to be compassionate *with your own money.* You're *not* free to be "compassionate" with someone else's.

The truth is that those pushing to expand old-age welfare programs have no right to claim they are compassionate. There is nothing compassionate about stifling economic growth and thereby sentencing more Americans to poverty. There is nothing compassionate about making the elderly dependent on welfare. There is nothing compassionate about drafting young people into debt and crushing their opportunities, hopes, and dreams.

For all their talk of compassion, the welfare state pushers are not really interested in helping people. If they were, they would be much more alarmed by the failure of the welfare state to lift people out of poverty, and they would be the most vocal champions of capitalism, which is the only system ever to create mass prosperity.

The Compassion Myth is not an argument but a *smear* designed to shame and silence those who dare question the welfare state. But we must question it. The welfare state is one of the cruelest, most inhumane, most immoral institutions ever devised. The most compassionate thing a person can do is fight for its abolition.

Ending the Debt Draft

During the Vietnam War, many defended the military draft using arguments virtually indistinguishable from those used to defend the Debt Draft. They said that Americans had a duty to serve society by fighting in the military. They said that the costs of a volunteer military would be too great. They said that only a draft could achieve national security. These arguments were plausible. Americans could not really project what the country would be like without a draft. But these arguments were false—and the institution they were used to defend was deeply immoral. The parallel to today's Debt Draft is exact.

In an individualist society, we prosper, we protect ourselves from risks, and we do it all without looting or exploiting others. Had we never created Social Security and Medicare, the elderly would not be impoverished—they would be enriched. And young Americans would not be starting their lives hundreds of thousands of dollars in debt.

There is no justification for the Debt Draft. There is no reason why young people should have to see their futures washed away in order to support older Americans. And there was no reason older Americans should have spent their youth carrying the burdens of *their* elders.

It's time to end our collectivist old-age welfare system and restore the free market and American individualism. In an individualist society, you have a right to exist for your own sake and deal with others on voluntary, mutually beneficial terms. You keep what you earn and you get to use it to pursue your goals and dreams. You are *not* your grandfather's keeper. No one has the right to be kept.

Our aim should not be to save Social Security and Medicare, or make them affordable, but to abolish them. They are inherently immoral programs that force some people to serve the goals and purposes of others. They are tools of exploitation.

To be sure, we should not get rid of these programs overnight. They must be *phased out* over time so that those who have been rendered dependent on the government have time to adjust and adapt. But the goal is clear. A moral society cannot tolerate turning its citizens into servants.

What can you do to fight the Debt Draft? Help wage a *moral crusade* against the collectivist ideas that have led to it. The welfare state cannot exist without the consent of its victims. It counts on the people being exploited to accept that they are being sacrificed for a noble cause. If the victims ever rebelled publicly and said they do *not* consent to being victimized—that the Debt Draft is *immoral*—then the whole thing would collapse.

Speak out for the individualist ideas this country was founded on. Tell the world that you are not the property of society and that your duty in life is not to pay for other people's retirement homes and hip replacements. You have a right to pursue your own happiness through your own independent effort.

Here are three small, simple steps you can take immediately.

1. **"Like" the End the Debt Draft Facebook Page.** Not only will this keep you up to date on our latest activities, but if we hit significant numbers, the world will know that there is a highly motivated group of Americans willing to stand up for their rights. Just visit www.facebook.com/debtdraft.

2. **Educate Yourself.** To win this fight, you must know your case. Start by visiting www.endthedebtdraft.com where you will find a ton of free resources that will leave you intellectually armed to the teeth and ready to fight the Debt Draft.

3. **Distribute Great Content.** We need to get our ideas heard. The highest leverage activity for most people is to find great content—persuasive books, articles, videos—and help them gain a wider audience. Start by distributing this pamphlet to your friends, family, and classmates.

During the Vietnam War, young Americans rallied against the military draft. Not all of them did so for honorable reasons. But there were some who recognized that your life belongs to you, not to others. It is time for a new student rebellion, a *moral* rebellion against welfare state exploitation.

ENDNOTES

1. In policy circles, "entitlements" has a technical meaning distinct from terms such as "welfare" and "welfare state." I regard the terms as synonymous.

2. See, for instance, Veronique de Rugy, "The U.S. Debt in Perspective," Mercatus Center, July 16, 2003, http://mercatus.org/publication/us-debt-perspective (accessed December 2, 2013). Even the lower-end estimates of the entitlement state's costs are terrifying—especially when you consider that historically we have tended to underestimate, not overestimate, those costs.

3. Laurence Kotlikoff, "Assessing Fiscal Sustainability," Mercatus Research, December 12, 2013, http://mercatus.org/sites/default/files/Kotlikoff_Fiscal Sustainability_v2.pdf (accessed April 5, 2014).

4. "CNN Poll: One in Five Say Social Security Is Unconstitutional," September 29, 2011, http://politicalticker.blogs.cnn.com/2011/09/29/cnn-poll-one-in-five-say-social-security-is-unconstitutional/ (accessed October 8, 2013).

5. "The Life of Julia," May 3, 2012, http://www.barackobama.com/truth-team/entry/the-life-of-julia/ (accessed October 8, 2013).

6. Dean Alfange, "Respectfully Quoted: A Dictionary of Quotations. 1989," Bartleby.com, http://www.bartleby.com/73/71.html (accessed January 18, 2014).

7. For more on the relationship between the Enlightenment and freedom, see the online course by my colleague Onkar Ghate, "The Morality of Freedom," at http://campus.aynrand.org/classroom/17/.

8. Thomas Jefferson, First Inaugural Address, Wednesday, March 4, 1801. Today we often hear that the Founding Fathers were supporters of *democracy*, including the majority's right to vote for entitlement programs. For a thorough analysis of the Founders' commitment to freedom, individual rights, and limited government, see Timothy Sandefur, *The Conscience of the Constitution* (Washington, DC: Cato, 2013).

9. Ralph Waldo Emerson, "Wealth," 1860, www.emersoncentral.com/wealth.htm (accessed October 8, 2013).

10. Matthew H. Smith, *Bulls and Bears of New York* (1873; reprint ed., Freeport, NY: Books for Libraries Press, 1972), p. 541.

11. H. A. Lewis, *Hidden Treasures* (Cleveland, OH: Moses, Lewis, & Co., 1888), pp. 490, 492.

12. Horatio Alger, preface to *Bound to Rise*, http://tinyurl.com/mq9dl9k (accessed October 8, 2013).

13. Daniel T. Rodgers, *The Work Ethic in Industrial America 1850–1920* (Chicago:

The University of Chicago Press, 1979), pp. 1–4.

14. Gordon S. Wood, *The Radicalism of the American Revolution* (New York: Vintage, 1992), p. 139.

15. J. Hector St. John de Crèvecœur, "Letters from an American Farmer: Letter III— What Is an American," http://avalon.law.yale.edu/18th_century/letter_03.asp (accessed November 22, 2013).

16. Rodgers, *The Work Ethic in Industrial America 1850–1920*, p. 5.

17. Daniel Yergin, *The Prize* (New York: Free Press, 2008), p. 15.

18. Alan Trachtenberg, *The Incorporation of America* (New York: Hill and Wang, 2007), p. 41.

19. "Centennial Exhibition Tours: Machinery Hall," http://libwww.library.phila. gov/CenCol/tours-machineryhall.htm (accessed October 8, 2013).

20. Francis J. Grund, *The Americans in Their Moral, Social, and Political Relations*, 2 vols. (London: Longman, Rees, Orme, Brown, Green and Longman, 1837), pp. 1–2, 5. Quoted in Rodgers, *The Work Ethic in Industrial America 1850–1920*, pp. 5–6.

21. Alexis de Tocqueville, "Of the Use That Americans Make of Association in Civil Life," *Democracy in America: Historical-Critical Edition of De la Démocratie en Amérique*, ed. Eduardo Nolla, trans. James T. Schleifer, vol. 3, part 2, chap. 5a. A Bilingual French-English Edition (Indianapolis: Liberty Fund, 2010), http://oll.libertyfund.org/title/2287/218996 (accessed February 2, 2014).

22. Wood, *The Radicalism of the American Revolution*, p. 328.

23. Ibid., p. 336.

24. Samuel Blodget, quoted in Wood, *The Radicalism of the American Revolution* pp. 338–39.

25. Ayn Rand, *Atlas Shrugged* (New York: Plume, 1999), p. 411.

26. Frederick Douglass, *My Bondage and My Freedom* (New York: Barnes & Noble Classics, 2005), p. 327.

27. Slavery was not the only example of how America fell short of the ideal of self-reliance and laissez-faire capitalism. For some of the ways government intervened in the economy during the nineteenth century, see William J. Novak, *The People's Welfare* (Chapel Hill: University of North Carolina Press, 1996).

28. Quoted in Jon Ward, "Paul Ryan Reads from 1850 Irish Government Poster to Make Case for Immigration Reform," *Huffington Post*, June 12, 2013, http://www.huffingtonpost.com/2013/06/12/paul-ryan-poster-irish-im_n_3428852.html (accessed October 8, 2013).

29. Eli Ginzberg, *The Unemployed* (New Brunswick: Transaction, 2010), p. 72.

30. Gertrude Himmelfarb, *The De-Moralization of Society* (New York: Vintage, 1996), p. 35.

31. James Bryce, *The American Commonwealth*, 3rd ed. (London: Macmillan, 1895), vol. 2, p. 369.

32. Massachusetts Bureau of Statistics (2013), pp. 1–2. *Annual Report on the Statistics of Labor, 1879* (Hong Kong: Forgotten Books: original work published 1879), pp. 126–27, https://play.google.com/store/books/details?id=QAUcAQAAIAAJ&r did=book-QAUcAQAAIAAJ&rdot=1 (accessed October 8, 2013).

33. Nicholas Eberstadt, "Are Entitlements Corrupting Us? Yes, American Character Is at Stake," *Wall Street Journal*, August 31, 2012, http://online.wsj.com/article/ SB10000872396390444914904577619671931313542.html (accessed October 8, 2013).

34. Thomas Babington Macaulay, *The History of England* (Philadelphia: John C. Winston Co., n.d.), vol. 3, p. 279.

35. Andrew Bernstein, *The Capitalist Manifesto* (New York: University Press of America, 2005), pp. 59–64.

36. Thomas J. Sugrue, "The Structures of Urban Poverty: The Reorganization of Space and Work in Three Periods of American History," in *The "Underclass" Debate: Views from History*, ed. Michael B. Katz (Princeton, NJ: Princeton University Press, 1993), p. 88.

37. Jack Larkin, *The Reshaping of Everyday Life: 1790–1840* (New York: Perennial Library, 1989), p. 74.

38. Ibid., p. 91

39. Gary M. Walton and Hugh Rockoff, *History of the American Economy*, 9th ed. (Toronto: Thomson Learning, 2002), p. 21.

40. Life Expectancy Graphs, http://mappinghistory.uoregon.edu/english/US/ US39-01.html (accessed on October 8, 2013).

41. W. Michael Cox and Richard Alm, *Myths of Rich and Poor* (New York: Basic Books, 1999), p. 55.

42. J. N. Kish, "U.S. Population 1776 to Present," https://www.google.com/fusion tables/DataSource?docid=1F1LWhYAo54sCTRkcnSJ1aZ8D9WUcEcxWlf26Ug (accessed October 8, 2013).

43. Kathryn M. Neckerman, "The Emergence of 'Underclass' Family Patterns, 1900–1940," in ed. Michael B. Katz, *The "Underclass" Debate* (Princeton: Princeton University Press, 1993), p. 206.

44. Quoted in Tamara K. Hareven, *Family Time & Industrial Time* (New York: Cambridge University Press, 1984), p. 259.

45. See, for instance, Stuart M. Blumin, *The Emergence of the Middle Class* (New York: Cambridge University Press, 1991), pp. 120–21.

46. Quoted in Napoleon Hill, *Think Your Way to Wealth* (New York: Tarcher/ Penguin, 2011), p. 12.

47. Richard Tedlow, *Giants of Enterprise* (New York: Collins, 2003), pp. 19–33. See also Don Watkins and Yaron Brook, "To Be Born Poor Doesn't Mean You'll

Always Be Poor," Forbes.com, April 12, 2013, http://www.forbes.com/sites/objectivist/2013/04/12/to-be-born-poor-doesnt-mean-youll-always-be-poor/ (accessed December 3, 2013).

48. Stuart M. Blumin, *The Emergence of the Middle Class* (New York: Cambridge University Press, 1991), p. 77.

49. Hareven, *Family Time & Industrial Time*, p. 121.

50. Ibid., pp. 69, 70, 77; George Reisman, *Capitalism* (Ottawa, IL: Jameson, 1998), p. 129.

51. See also my five-part blog series, "The Welfare State Myth," at http://ari.aynrand.org/blog/2014/04/03/the-welfare-state-myth-part-5 (accessed April 5, 2014).

52. Carolyn L. Weaver, *The Crisis in Social Security: Economic and Political Origins* (Durham, NC: Duke Press Policy Studies, 1982), p. 44.

53. Eli Ginzberg, *The Unemployed* (New Brunswick: Transaction, 2010), p. 29. All of the participants in the study had been unemployed for some stretch during the Depression, which suggests that among the population as a whole, the rates were even higher. See also Weaver, *The Crisis in Social Security*, pp. 46–47.

54. Steven Mintz and Susan Kellogg, *Domestic Revolutions* (New York: Free Press, 1988), p. 92.

55. David T. Beito, *From Mutual Aid to the Welfare State: Fraternal Societies and Social Services, 1890–1967* (Chapel Hill: University of North Carolina Press, 2000), p. 204. See also John Chodes, "Friendly Societies: Voluntary Social Security and More," *The Freeman*, March 1, 1990, http://www.fee.org/the_freeman/detail/friendly-societies-voluntary-social-security-and-more#axzz2WhNWtgjB (accessed October 20, 2013).

56. Beito, *From Mutual Aid to the Welfare State*, pp. 12–14.

57. See, for instance, Walter I. Trattner, *From Poor Law to Welfare State: A History of Social Welfare in America* (New York: Free Press, 1994), pp. 92–93, and Neckerman, "The Emergence of 'Underclass' Family Patterns, 1900–1940," in ed. Katz, *The "Underclass" Debate*, p. 202.

58. Trattner, *From Poor Law to Welfare State*, pp. 92–93.

59. *Historical Statistics of the United States*, vol. 2, part B, Work and Welfare, p. 2–865, http://www.hks.harvard.edu/fs/phall/HSUS.pdf (accessed January 18, 2014).

60. Marvin Olasky, *The Tragedy of American Compassion* (Washington, DC: Regnery, 1992), p. 149.

61. Robert H. Bremner, *American Philanthropy*, 2nd ed. (Chicago: University of Chicago Press, 1988), p. 133.

62. Richard K. Vedder and Lowell E. Gallaway, *Out of Work* (New York: New York University Press, 1997), pp. 53–54.

63. J. R. Vernon, "Unemployment Rates in Postbellum America: 1869–1899," *Journal*

of Macroeconomics 16, no. 4 (Autumn 1994), pp. 701–714, http://dx.doi.org/
10.1016/0164-0704(94)90008-6 (accessed October 24, 2013). Some earlier
estimates by other scholars put the rates somewhat higher. It should also
be noted that these downturns were arguably the result of government
intervention in the economy. Had America been fully capitalist, there is no
reason to think there would be sustained and widespread unemployment.
See, for instance, George Reisman, *Capitalism* (Ottawa, IL: Jameson, 1998),
pp. 580–94, 658–61, 938–42. As for the cause of nineteenth-century
financial panics, see George Selgin, "Misunderstanding Financial History,"
Free Banking blog, July 11, 2013, http://www.freebanking.org/2013/07/11/
misunderstanding-financial-history/ (accessed April 5, 2014).

64. Department of Homeland Security, "Yearbook of Immigration Statistics:
2010," http://www.dhs.gov/yearbook-immigration-statistics-2010-3 (accessed
December 3, 2013).

65. W. Andrew Achenbaum, *Old Age in the New Land* (Baltimore: Johns Hopkins
University Press, 1978), p. 85.

66. Roy Lubove, *The Struggle for Social Security: 1900–1935* (Pittsburgh: University of
Pittsburgh Press, 1986), p. 118. Original report: http://ia700303.us.archive.org/
26/items/cu31924032467841/cu31924032467841.pdf. Out of 177,000
residents sixty-five or older, 135,788 are listed as non-dependents; 27,230
of the remaining 41,212 received government (usually military) pensions.
Carolyn L. Weaver, *The Crisis in Social Security: Economic and Political Origins*
(Durham, NC: Duke Press Policy Studies, 1982), p. 42. For London
figures, see *The Poor Law Report of 1909*, chap. 3, https://archive.org/details/
poorlawreportof00bosaiala (accessed February 1, 2014).

67. John Myles, *Old Age in the Welfare State* (Lawrence, KS: University Press of
Kansas, 1989), pp. 8, 14.

68. Achenbaum, *Old Age in the New Land*, pp. 69–72. Rates did decrease somewhat
in the decades that followed, although Achenbaum argues for reasons other
than industrialization. See pages 74 and 105.

69. Lubove, *The Struggle for Social Security*, p. 13. See also Carolyn L. Weaver, *The
Crisis in Social Security: Economic and Political Origins* (Durham, NC: Duke Press
Policy Studies, 1982), pp. 47–49.

70. Achenbaum, *Old Age in the New Land*, p. 82.

71. Daniel Béland, *Social Security: History and Politics from the New Deal to the
Privatization Debate* (Lawrence, KS: University Press of Kansas, 2005), p. 50, and
Lubove, *The Struggle for Social Security*, pp. 133–34. By 1921, this had dropped to
less than 1 percent. See Weaver, *The Crisis in Social Security* p. 30.

72. Olasky, *The Tragedy of American Compassion*, p. 8.

73. Deut. 15:7–8 (NIV).

74. Hace Sorel Tishler, *Self-Reliance and Social Security: 1870–1917* (Port
Washington, NY: National University Publications, 1971), p. 67.

75. Michael Tanner, *The End of Welfare* (Washington, DC: Cato, 1996), p. 37.

76. Achenbaum, *Old Age in the New Land*, p. 83.

77. W. Andrew Achenbaum, *Social Security: Visions and Revisions* (New York: Cambridge University Press, 1986), p 19.

78. Franklin D. Roosevelt, "Message to Congress Reviewing the Broad Objectives and Accomplishments of the Administration," June 8, 1934, http://www.ssa .gov/history/fdrcon34.html (accessed October 20, 2013).

79. Ronald J. Pestritto and William J. Atto, *American Progressivism: A Reader* (New York: Lexington, 2008), pp. 1–3.

80. Herbert Croly, *The Promise of American Life* (New York: Macmillan, 1909), p. 36.

81. William Blackstone, "Property: William Blackstone, Commentaries 1:134– 35, 140–41," 1765, http://press-pubs.uchicago.edu/founders/documents/ v1ch16s5.html (accessed October 20, 2013).

82. "From the Archives: President Teddy Roosevelt's New Nationalism Speech," August 31, 1910, http://www.whitehouse.gov/blog/2011/12/06/archives-president-teddy-roosevelts-new-nationalism-speech (accessed October 20, 2013).

83. Quoted in Ronald J. Pestritto, *Woodrow Wilson and the Roots of Modern Liberalism* (Lanham, MD: Rowman and Littlefield, 2005), p. 255.

84. Quoted in Jonah Goldberg, *Liberal Fascism* (New York, Doubleday, 2007), p. 86.

85. Croly, *The Promise of American Life*, p. 22.

86. Ayn Rand, *For the New Intellectual* (New York: Signet, 1963), p. 43.

87. Nancy J. Altman, *The Battle for Social Security* (Hoboken, NJ: Wiley, 2005), p. 9.

88. Carolyn L. Weaver, *The Crisis in Social Security: Economic and Political Origins* (Durham, NC: Duke Press Policy Studies, 1982), p. 37.

89. Quoted in Larry W. DeWitt, Daniel Béland, and Edward D. Berkowitz, *Social Security: A Document History* (Washington, DC: CQ Press, 2008), p. 32.

90. Ibid., p. 34.

91. Ibid., pp. 35–6.

92. Weaver, *The Crisis in Social Security*, p. 36.

93. Daniel Béland, *Social Security: History and Politics from the New Deal to the Privatization Debate* (Lawrence, KS: Kansas, 2005), 61.

94. See Leonard Peikoff, *The Ominous Parallels* (New York: Meridian, 1993), especially chapters 5 and 14.

95. Quoted in Marvin Olasky, *The Tragedy of American Compassion* (Washington, DC: Regnery, 1992), p. 163.

96. Ibid., p. 163.

97.   Quoted in DeWitt et al., *Social Security: A Document History*, p. 82.

98.   Thomas J. Sugrue, "The Structures of Urban Poverty: The Reorganization of Space and Work in Three Periods of American History," in *The "Underclass" Debate: Views from History*, ed. Michael B. Katz (Princeton, NJ: Princeton University Press, 1993), p. 95.

99.   Franklin D. Roosevelt, "Message to Congress Reviewing the Broad Objectives and Accomplishments of the Administration," June 8, 1934, http://www.ssa .gov/history/fdrcon34.html (accessed October 20, 2013).

100. See, for instance, Tamara K. Hareven, *Family Time & Industrial Time* (New York: Cambridge, 1984).

101. Walter I. Trattner, *From Poor Law to Welfare State: A History of Social Welfare in America* (New York: Free Press, 1994), p. 92.

102. For more on this issue, see George Selgin, William D. Lastrapes, and Lawrence H. White, "Has the Fed Been a Failure?" Cato Working Paper, December 2010, http://www.cato.org/sites/cato.org/files/pubs/pdf/WorkingPaper-2.pdf (accessed October 23, 2013); Lawrence W. Reed, "Great Myths of the Great Depression," January 1, 1998, http://www.mackinac.org/4013 (accessed March 22, 2011); Burton W. Folsom, Jr., *New Deal or Raw Deal? FDR's Economic Legacy Has Damaged America* (New York: Threshold, 2008); Lawrence H. White, *The Clash of Economic Ideas* (New York: Cambridge, 2012), pp. 68–154; and Amity Shlaes, *The Forgotten Man: A New History of the Great Depression* (New York: Harper Perennial, 2008).

103. Clarence B. Carson, *The Welfare State: 1929–1985* (Wadley, AL: American Textbook Committee, 1994), p. 63.

104. Ibid., pp. 62–65.

105. William Voegeli, *Never Enough: America's Limitless Welfare State* (New York: Encounter Books, 2010), pp. 69–70.

106. Achenbaum, *Social Security: Visions and Revisions*, p. 35.

107. Quoted in DeWitt et al., *Social Security: A Document History*, pp. 94, 97. The parallels between Landon's failed argument and the recent campaign by American Enterprise Institute president Arthur Brooks for "a conservative social-justice agenda" are striking. See Arthur Brooks, "Be Open-Handed Toward Your Brothers," *Commentary*, February 2014, http://www.commentarymagazine.com/ article/be-open-handed-toward-your-brothers-1/ (accessed April 5, 2014).

108. Trattner, *From Poor Law to Welfare State*, p. 296.

109. W. Andrew Achenbaum, *Social Security: Visions and Revisions* (New York: Cambridge University Press, 1986), p. 25.

110. Social Security Administration, Research Note #23, "Luther Gulick Memorandum re: Famous FDR Quote," http://www.ssa.gov/history/Gulick. html (accessed October 22, 2013).

111. "The 1936 Government Pamphlet on Social Security," http://www.ssa.gov/ history/ssn/ssb36.html (accessed October 22, 2013).

112. "A Message on Social Security to Congress, January 17, 1935," in *FDR Public Papers*, vol. 4, p. 44, http://www.ssa.gov/history/pdf/hr35pres.pdf (accessed October 22, 2013).

113. Research Notes & Special Studies by the Historian's Office, "Research Note #3: Details of Ida May Fuller's Payroll Tax Contributions," http://www.ssa.gov/history/idapayroll.html (accessed December 4, 2013).

114. Sylvester J. Schieber and John B. Shoven, *The Real Deal: The History and Future of Social Security* (New Haven, CT: Yale University Press, 1999), p. 47.

115. "James Madison to James Robertson, Jr.," April 20, 1831, http://rotunda.upress.virginia.edu/founders/default.xqy?keys=FOEA-print-02-02-02-2332 (accessed October 22, 2013).

116. Schieber and Shoven, *The Real Deal*, p. 48.

117. Charlotte A. Twight, *Dependent on D.C.: The Rise of Federal Control over the Lives of Ordinary Americans* (New York: Palgrave, 2002), pp. 87–88.

118. Quoted in Twight, *Dependent on D.C.*, pp. 68–69.

119. Ibid., p. 68.

120. A Ponzi scheme, according to the U.S. Securities and Exchange Commission, is "an investment fraud that involves the payment of purported returns to existing investors from funds contributed by new investors. Ponzi scheme organizers often solicit new investors by promising to invest funds in opportunities claimed to generate high returns with little or no risk. In many Ponzi schemes, the fraudsters focus on attracting new money to make promised payments to earlier-stage investors to create the false appearance that investors are profiting from a legitimate business." See U.S. Securities and Exchange Commission, "Ponzi Schemes," http://www.sec.gov/answers/ponzi.htm (accessed December 4, 2013).

121. Quoted in Schieber and Shoven, *The Real Deal*, p. 110.

122. Ibid.

123. Achenbaum, *Social Security: Visions and Revisions*, p. 36.

124. Franklin D. Roosevelt, "State of the Union Message to Congress," January 11, 1944, http://www.fdrlibrary.marist.edu/archives/address_text.html (accessed October 22, 2013).

125. Ibid.

126. Clarence B. Carson, *The Welfare State: 1929–1985* (Wadley, AL: American Textbook Committee, 1994), p. 184.

127. Marvin Olasky, *The Tragedy of American Compassion* (Washington, DC: Regnery, 1992), p. 152.

128. Ibid., p. 154.

129. Thomas Jefferson, "Manufactures," *Notes on the State of Virginia*.

130. Quoted in Charles Murray, *Coming Apart* (New York: Crown Forum, 2012), p.

132.

131. Quoted in Olasky, *The Tragedy of American Compassion*, p. 165.

132. Mario A. Pei, "The America We Lost," *The Freeman*, March 1996, pp. 132–33.

133. William H. Whyte, *The Organization Man* (Philadelphia: University of Pennsylvania Press, 2002), p. 7.

134. David Riesman, "The Uncommitted Generation" in *The American Gospel of Success*, ed. Moses Rischin (Chicago: Quadrangle, 1968), pp. 375–76, 374.

135. Whyte, *The Organization Man*, p. 5.

136. As one very rough measure, mentions of "self-reliant" in books first rise to prominence in the late nineteenth century and remain high through 1920, after which they decline significantly until the late 1970s. http://books.google.com/ngrams/graph?content=self-reliant&year_start=1800&year_end=2000&corpus=15&smoothing=1&share=.

137. Quoted in Olasky, *The Tragedy of American Compassion*, p. 18.

138. Olasky, *The Tragedy of American Compassion*, pp. 165–74.

139. Sylvester J. Schieber and John B. Shoven, *The Real Deal: The History and Future of Social Security* (New Haven, CT: Yale University Press, 1999), pp. 149–52.

140. Quoted in W. Andrew Achenbaum, *Social Security: Visions and Revisions* (New York: Cambridge University Press, 1986), p. 54.

141. Ibid., p. 55.

142. That there were certain challenges faced by the elderly when it came to getting medical insurance was true. But these problems were created by the government. In particular, the government had made health insurance purchased through one's employer tax deductible, and by the 1960s, many Americans were covered under employer-sponsored plans. The trouble was that many Americans would eventually retire: At a time when their health risks were highest, elderly Americans found themselves having to purchase new health plans at rates far above what they had been paying. The government could have repealed the tax exemption for employers or expanded it to include individually purchased health insurance. Instead, the entitlement statists used a problem created by government intervention to urge further government intervention: government-provided health insurance for the elderly.

143. Sue A. Blevins, *Medicare's Midlife Crisis* (Washington, DC: Cato, 2001), p. 42. There were also a number of state and federal government programs to assist the elderly in getting medical care, notably the means-tested Kerr-Mills program.

144. Robert M. Ball, "What Medicare's Architects Had in Mind," *Health Affairs* 14, no. 4 (Winter 1995), http://www.theinsidereport.org/FamilyHeritage/Arthur%20Hess/Perceptions%20on%20Medicare.pdf (accessed October 22, 2013). See also Leonard Peikoff, "Medicine: The Death of a Profession," in Ayn Rand, *The Voice of Reason* (New York: Meridian, 1990).

145. Shirley Scheibla, *Poverty Is Where the Money Is* (New York: Arlington House, 1968), p. 102.

146. Quoted in Irwin Unger, *The Best of Intentions* (New York: Doubleday, 1996), p. 177.

147. Ibid., p. 178.

148. Scheibla, *Poverty Is Where the Money Is*, pp. 103–4, http://www.davemanuel.com/median-household-income.php (Census website down).

149. Achenbaum, *Social Security: Visions and Revisions*, p. 56.

150. Olasky, *The Tragedy of American Compassion*, p. 175.

151. Ibid., p. 178.

152. Quoted in James A. Dorn, "The Rise of Government and the Decline of Morality," *The Freeman*, March 1996, p. 137.

153. Walter E. Williams, *Up From the Projects* (Stanford, CA: Hoover Institution Press, 2010), p. 7.

154. James Gwartney and Thomas S. McCaleb, "Have Antipoverty Programs Increased Poverty?" *Cato Journal* 5, no. 1 (Spring/Summer 1985), http://object.cato.org/sites/cato.org/files/serials/files/cato-journal/1985/5/cj5n1-1.pdf (accessed April 7, 2014).

155. Olasky, *The Tragedy of American Compassion*, pp. 168–69.

156. Quoted in Charles J. Sykes, *A Nation of Moochers* (New York: St. Martin's Press, 2011), p. 46.

157. Olasky, *The Tragedy of American Compassion*, pp. 182–83.

158. Thomas J. Sugrue, "The Structures of Urban Poverty: The Reorganization of Space and Work in Three Periods of American History," in *The "Underclass" Debate: Views from History*, ed. Michael B. Katz (Princeton, NJ: Princeton University Press, 1993), p. 88.

159. The other half of the tragedy is that the government has been putting roadblocks in the way of the *ambitious* poor. Not only burdensome payroll taxes, but minimum wage laws, expensive permits and licensing requirements for new businesses, and other such barriers make it harder and harder for poor people to lift themselves out of poverty. And this is to say nothing of the deplorable educational opportunities available to low-income individuals thanks to the government school system.

160. Achenbaum, *Social Security: Visions and Revisions*, p. 59.

161. W. Andrew Achenbaum, *Social Security: Visions and Revisions* (New York: Cambridge University Press, 1986), p. 62.

162. Sylvester J. Schieber and John B. Shoven, *The Real Deal: The History and Future of Social Security* (New Haven, CT: Yale University Press, 1999), p. 184.

163. Charles Blahous, *Social Security: The Unfinished Work* (Stanford, CA: Hoover Institution Press, 2010), p. 33. There is some evidence that the Social Security Administration senior executives knew the benefit formula would lead rates

to skyrocket, yet went ahead anyway out of a desire to raise Social Security benefits relative to wages. For more on this episode, see Schieber and Shoven, *The Real Deal*, pp. 166–82.

164. Ayn Rand, "Collectivized Ethics," *The Virtue of Selfishness* (New York: Signet, 1964), p. 94.

165. Ibid., p. 95. See also Yaron Brook and Don Watkins, *Free Market Revolution: How Ayn Rand's Ideas Can End Big Government* (New York: Palgrave, 2012).

166. See, for instance, F. A. Hayek, *The Road to Serfdom* (Chicago: University of Chicago Press, 1994), and Milton Friedman, *Capitalism and Freedom* (Chicago: University of Chicago Press, 1982).

167. Schieber and Shoven, *The Real Deal*, pp. 202–3.

168. Some commentators have tried to defend the economic meaningfulness of the trust fund. For a thorough debunking of their arguments, see Blahous, *Social Security: The Unfinished Work*, pp. 51–60. See also Schieber and Shoven, *The Real Deal*, pp. 203–7.

169. William J. Clinton, "Remarks by the President on Social Security—1993–1998," Gaston Hall, Georgetown University, February 9, 1998, http://www.ssa.gov/history/clntstmts.html#Gaston (accessed October 22, 2013).

170. Michael D. Tanner, "Clinton Wanted Social Security Privatized," July 13, 2001, http://www.cato.org/publications/commentary/clinton-wanted-social-security-privatized (accessed December 4, 2013). Clinton's overall entitlement record is mixed. In his first term, he attempted an ambitious government takeover of medicine, popularly known as "HillaryCare," after his wife. But Clinton also vowed to "end welfare as we know it," and passed a welfare reform measure in 1996 that marginally lessened the destructive effects of the welfare system. For a fascinating account of this latter episode, see Jason DeParle, *American Dream* (New York: Penguin, 2005).

171. Blahous, *Social Security: The Unfinished Work*, p. 207.

172. George W. Bush, "The President and Social Security Reform," January 11, 2005, http://www.presidentialrhetoric.com/speeches/01.11.05.html (accessed November 28, 2013).

173. Terry Gross, "Looking at President Bush, Seeing an 'Impostor,'" *National Public Radio*, February 22, 2006, http://www.npr.org/templates/story/story.php?storyId =5227215 (accessed October 22, 2013).

174. "Transcript and Audio: Second Presidential Debate," October 16, 2012, http://www.npr.org/2012/10/16/163050988/transcript-obama-romney-2nd-presidential-debate (accessed October 22, 2013).

175. Devin Dwyer, "Obama: If We Lose in 2012, Government Will Tell People 'You're On Your Own,'" October 26, 2011, http://abcnews.go.com/blogs/politics/2011/10/obama-if-we-lose-in-2012-government-will-tell-people-youre-on-your-own/ (accessed October 22, 2013).

176. Caroline May, "USDA Combats 'Mountain Pride' Self-reliance to Boost Food Stamp Rolls," July 3, 2012, http://dailycaller.com/2012/07/03/usda-combats-mountain-pride-self-reliance-to-boost-food-stamp-rolls/ (accessed October 22, 2013).

177. "Franklin Roosevelt's Statement on Signing the Social Security Act," August 14, 1935, http://docs.fdrlibrary.marist.edu/odssast.html (accessed October 22, 2013).

178. Franklin D. Roosevelt, "State of the Union Message to Congress," January 11, 1944, http://www.fdrlibrary.marist.edu/archives/address_text.html (accessed October 22, 2013).

179. Geoffrey Dickens, "Flashback: Pelosi Responds with 'Are You Serious?' to Question about ObamaCare's Constitutionality," March 26, 2012, http://newsbusters.org/blogs/geoffrey-dickens/2012/03/26/flashback-pelosi-responds-are-you-serious-question-about-obamacare (accessed December 5, 2013).

180. Ezra Klein, "Elizabeth Warren Wants to Spend More on Social Security. But She's Not Thinking Big Enough!" *Wonkblog*, November 19, 2013, http://www.washingtonpost.com/blogs/wonkblog/wp/2013/11/19/elizabeth-warren-wants-to-spend-more-on-social-security-but-shes-not-thinking-big-enough/ (accessed November 24, 2013).

181. Social Security Administration, "Frequently Asked Questions," http://www.ssa.gov/history/hfaq.html (accessed October 23, 2013). Christopher Chantrill, "Social Security as Pct GDP," http://www.usgovernmentspending.com/spending_chart_1935_2015USp_XXs6li011mcn_01f02f_Social_Security_as_Pct_GDP (accessed October 23, 2013).

182. Nicholas Eberstadt, introduction to "The Rise of Entitlements in Modern America, 1960–2010,"*A Nation of Takers: America's Entitlement Epidemic* (West Conshohocken, PA: Templeton, 2012).

183. Tom Wolfe, "Sorry, But Your Soul Just Died," OrthodoxyToday.org, 1996, http://www.orthodoxytoday.org/articles/Wolfe-Sorry-But-Your-Soul-Just-Died.php (accessed October 23, 2013).

184. Laurence J. Kotlikoff and Scott Burns, *The Clash of Generations* (Cambridge, MA: MIT Press, 2012), chapter 1.

185. Medicaid is targeted toward low-income Americans of all ages, but most Medicaid spending is directed toward the elderly. "Total Personal Health Care Spending, By Age Group, Calendar Years, 1987, 1996, 1999, 2002, 2004," CMS.gov, http://www.cms.gov/Research-Statistics-Data-and-Systems/Statistics-Trends-and-Reports/NationalHealthExpendData/Downloads/2004-age-tables.pdf (accessed December 5, 2013).

186. "The 2013 Annual Report of the Board of Trustees of the Federal Old-Age and Survivors Insurance and Federal Disability Insurance Trust Funds," May 31, 2013, http://www.socialsecurity.gov/oact/tr/2013/tr2013.pdf (accessed October 23, 2013). These are "infinite horizon" values. There are shorter-term (seventy-five year) cost estimates, but they too do not tell the

whole story, since they effectively treat incoming payroll taxes as government assets. However, these "assets" can also be viewed as liabilities, since they represent future claims to entitlement benefits.

187. Giovanni Callegari and Laurence J. Kotlikoff, "Estimating the U.S. 2013 Fiscal Gap," The Can Kicks Back, http://www.thecankicksback.org/2013_fiscal_gap (accessed February 5, 2014).

188. See also Jeffrey Rogers Hummel, "Some Possible Consequences of a U.S. Government Default," *Econ Journal Watch* 9, no.1 (January 2012), http://econjwatch.org/articles/some-possible-consequences-of-a-us-government-default (accessed October 23, 2013).

189. Elise Gould, "Social Security Is the Most Effective Anti-Poverty Program in the U.S., in One Chart," *The Economic Policy Institute Blog*, July 30, 2013, http://www.epi.org/blog/social-security-effective-anti-poverty-program/ (accessed November 28, 2013).

190. Carmen DeNavas-Walt, Bernadette D. Proctor, Jessica C. Smith, "Income, Poverty, and Health Insurance Coverage in the United States: 2012, United States Census Bureau," http://www.census.gov/prod/2013pubs/p60-245.pdf (accessed December 6, 2013).

191. Laurence J. Kotlikoff and Scott Burns, *The Clash of Generations* (Cambridge, MA: MIT Press, 2012), chap. 1. See also Jagadeesh Gokhale, Lawrence J. Kotlikoff, John Sabelhaus, "Understanding the Postwar Decline in U.S. Savings: A Cohort Analysis," NBER Working Paper Series, Working Paper 5571, May 1996, http://people.bu.edu/kotlikof/PostwarSaving.pdf (accessed November 21, 2013).

192. See "Egalitarianism and Inflation" in Ayn Rand, *Philosophy Who Needs It* (New York: Signet, 1984), and "The Inverted Moral Priorities" in Ayn Rand, *The Voice of Reason* (New York: Meridian, 1990).

193. Kotlikoff and Burns, *The Clash of Generations*, chap. 4.

194. Edgar K. Browning, *Stealing from Each Other* (Westport, CT: Praeger, 2008), p. x. Emphasis in original.

195. Ibid., pp. 116–17.

196. Harry Binswanger, "The Meaning of Social Security," Harry Binswanger List, November 26, 2012, http://www.hblist.com.

197. George Selgin, William D. Lastrapes, and Lawrence H. White, "Has the Fed Been a Failure?" Cato Working Paper, December 2010, http://www.cato.org/sites/cato.org/files/pubs/pdf/WorkingPaper-2.pdf (accessed October 23, 2013).

198. Nicholas Eberstadt, introduction to "The Rise of Entitlements in Modern America, 1960–2010," *A Nation of Takers: America's Entitlement Epidemic* (West Conshohocken, PA: Templeton Press, 2012).

199. For more on the 1950s canard, see Brink Lindsey, "Paul Krugman's Nostalgianomics: Economic Policies, Social Norms, and Income Inequality,"

Cato Institute White Paper, February 9, 2009, http://object.cato.org/sites/
cato.org/files/pubs/pdf/Nostalgianomics.pdf (accessed November 24, 2013);
James Pethokoukis, "Why We Can't Go Back to Sky-high, 1950s Tax Rates,"
AEI Ideas, April 18, 2012, http://www.aei-ideas.org/2012/04/why-we-cant-
go-back-to-sky-high-1950s-tax-rates/ (accessed November 24, 2013); and
Peter Schiff, "The Fantasy of a 91% Top Income Tax Rate," *Wall Street Journal*,
December 6, 2012, http://online.wsj.com/article/SB10001424127887324705 1
04578151601554982808.html (accessed November 24, 2013).

200. Frederick Douglass, *Narrative of the Life of Frederick Douglass: An American Slave*
      (New York: Bedford, 1993), p. 95.

201. *Washington Post* (October 29, 1982, p. A28). Thanks to Peter Schwartz for
      bringing this quote to my attention.

202. Ayn Rand, "A Preview–Part II," *Ayn Rand Letter*, vol. 1, no. 22, July 31, 1972.

203. Theodore Dalrymple, *Life at the Bottom* (Chicago: Ivan R. Dee, 2001), p. 138.

204. Ibid., p. 142.

205. "Bono: Only Capitalism Can End Poverty," The Inquisitr, December 7, 2012,
      http://www.inquisitr.com/428836/bono-only-capitalism-can-end-poverty-
      video/ (accessed October 23, 2013).

206. Brian Leiter, interview by Richard Marshall, "leiter reports," *3:AM Magazine*,
      December 19, 2011, http://www.3ammagazine.com/3am/leiter-reports/
      (accessed October 23, 2013).

207. Quoted in Arthur Brooks, *The Road to Freedom* (New York: Basic Books, 2012),
      p. 56.

208. See Ayn Rand, *Atlas Shrugged* (New York: Plume, 1999), pp. 1035–40; Ayn
      Rand, "The Age of Envy," *Return of the Primitive* (New York: Meridian, 1999),
      pp. 130–58; and Ayn Rand, "The Monument Builders," *The Virtue of Selfishness*
      (New York: Signet, 1964), pp. 100–107.

209. Quoted in Brooks, *The Road to Freedom*, p. 62.

210. Marshall Cohen, review of *A Theory of Justice*, by John Rawls, *New York Times*,
      July 16, 1972. Quoted in Leonard Peikoff, *The DIM Hypothesis* (New York: New
      American Library, 2012), p. 177.

211. Michael Harrington, *The Other America: Poverty in the United States* (New York:
      Touchstone, 1997), p. 178.

212. Quoted in Larry W. DeWitt, Daniel Béland, and Edward D. Berkowitz, *Social
      Security: A Document History* (Washington, DC: CQ Press, 2008), p. 34. Christian
      thinkers have indeed long treated self-reliance as one of the worst vices: a
      form of pride. See for instance, Seth Lobis, "'Self-Reliance': The Prehistory of
      Emerson's Famous Word," *In Character*, January 1, 2007, http://incharacter.org/
      archives/self-reliance/self-reliance-the-prehistory-of-emersons-famous-word/
      (accessed October 23, 2013). As a result, most have opposed the self-reliant
      society and supported the entitlement state in some form.

213. See Yaron Brook and Don Watkins, *Free Market Revolution: How Ayn Rand's*

Ideas Can End Big Government (New York: Palgrave, 2012), pp. 81–84.

214. Rand, *Atlas Shrugged*, pp. 1031–32. See also my interview with Onkar Ghate on the morality of the welfare state, available at http://ari.aynrand.org/blog/2014/04/01/the-debt-dialogues-episode-4-onkar-ghate-on-the-morality-of-the-welfare-state (accessed April 5, 2014).

215. Ayn Rand, "The Objectivist Ethics," *The Virtue of Selfishness* (New York: Signet, 1964), pp. 34–35.

216. See Brook and Watkins, *Free Market Revolution*, pp. 124–35.

217. "Inspirational Man Born with No Arms Drives His [Impala] and Works for NASCAR Racing Team!," September 2, 2013, http://www.youtube.com/watch?v=usuQAYE2ASo (accessed November 22, 2013).

218. Ben Carson with Cecil Murphey, *Gifted Hands: The Ben Carson Story* (Grand Rapids, MI: Zondervan, 1990), p. 37.

219. Ibid., pp. 63–64.

220. Ibid., p. 103.

221. Ibid., p. 106.

222. Ibid., p. 117.

223. Alex Epstein, "I've Got a Business—and I Built It," July 19, 2012, http://industrialprogress.com/2012/07/19/ive-got-a-business-and-i-built-it/ (accessed October 23, 2013).

224. Quoted in Sylvester J. Schieber, *The Predictable Surprise: The Unraveling of the U.S Retirement System* (New York: Oxford University Press, 2012), p. 45. For more on this, see Charles Blahous, *Social Security: The Unfinished Work* (Stanford, CA: Hoover Institution Press, 2010), pp. 123–36.

225. Jonathan Peterson, *Social Security for Dummies* (Hoboken, NJ: Wiley, 2012), p. 18.

226. Krzysztof M. Ostaszewski, "Privatizing the Social Security Trust Fund? Don't Let the Government Invest," January 14, 1997, Cato Institute, http://www.cato.org/publications/social-security-choice-paper/privatizing-social-security-trust-fund-dont-let-government-invest (accessed October 23, 2013).

227. Ayn Rand, *The Fountainhead* (New York: Signet, 1943), p. 683.

228. Ayn Rand, *Atlas Shrugged* (New York: Plume, 1999), pp. 1027–33. See also Yaron Brook and Don Watkins, *Free Market Revolution: How Ayn Rand's Ideas Can End Big Government* (New York: Palgrave, 2012), pp. 81–85.

229. Bettina Bien Greaves, "Henry Hazlitt: A Man for Many Seasons," *The Freeman*, November 1, 1989, http://www.fee.org/the_freeman/detail/henry-hazlitt-a-man-for-many-seasons#axzz2a5gcTkVN (accessed October 24, 2013).

230. Ayn Rand, *The Voice of Reason* (New York: Meridian, 1990), p. 42.

231. Laurence Kotlikoff, "Assessing Fiscal Sustainability," The Mercatus Center, December 12, 2013, http://mercatus.org/publication/assessing-fiscal-sustainability (accessed January 21, 2014).

232. Laurence J. Kotlikoff and Scott Burns, *The Clash of Generations* (Cambridge, MA: MIT Press, 2012), chap. 1.

233. Thomas Jefferson, prospectus for his translation of Destutt de Tracy's *Treatise on Political Economy*, communicated to Joseph Milligan in a letter of April 6, 1816, http://www.monticello.org/site/jefferson/democracy-will-cease-to-exist-quotation (accessed January 18, 2014).

234. All figures from usgovernmentspending.com.

235. Quoted in Jonah Goldberg, *Liberal Fascism* (New York: Doubleday, 2007), p. 86.

236. Ayn Rand, *The Virtue of Selfishness* (New York: Signet, 1964), p. 149.

237. Herbert Croly, *The Promise of American Life* (New York: Macmillan, 1909), p. 22.

238. "U.S. Health Plans Have History of Cost Overruns," *Washington Times*, November 18, 2009, http://www.washingtontimes.com/news/2009/nov/18/health-programs-have-history-of-cost-overruns/?page=all (accessed January 21, 2014); "Medicare Spending and Financing Fact Sheet," The Henry J. Kaiser Family Foundation, November 14, 2012, http://kff.org/medicare/fact-sheet/medicare-spending-and-financing-fact-sheet/ (accessed January 21, 2014). See also Yaron Brook and Don Watkins, *Free Market Revolution: How Ayn Rand's Ideas Can End Big Government* (New York: Palgrave, 2013), chap. 13.

239. "Social Security and Medicare Tax Rates," Social Security Online, http://www.ssa.gov/OACT/ProgData/taxRates.html (accessed January 21, 2014). Actually, this is an understatement. It includes only payroll taxes, but a substantial portion of Medicare is funded through the government's general tax revenues, such as income taxes.

240. "Generational Equity Slides, Stan Druckenmiller," YouTube video, October 26, 2013, http://www.youtube.com/watch?v=fb2Qd89trbQ (accessed February 1, 2014).

241. Daniel J. Mitchell, "The War on Poverty Has Been a Disaster for Taxpayers … and for Poor People," January 8, 2014, http://danieljmitchell.wordpress.com/2014/01/08/the-war-on-poverty-has-been-a-disaster-for-taxpayers-and-for-poor-people/ (accessed January 21, 2014).

242. Laurence J. Kotlikoff and Scott Burns, *The Clash of Generations* (Cambridge, MA: MIT Press, 2012), chap. 1.

243. Edgar K. Browning, *Stealing from Each Other* (Westport, CT: Praeger, 2008), p. x.

244. Sue A. Blevins, *Medicare's Midlife Crisis* (Washington, DC: Cato, 2001), pp. 7–9, 69–70.

245. Walter I. Trattner, *From Poor Law to Welfare State: A History of Social Welfare in America* (New York: Free Press, 1994), pp. 92–93.

246. W. Andrew Achenbaum, *Old Age in the New Land* (Baltimore: Johns Hopkins University Press, 1978), p. 85.

ABOUT THE AUTHOR

Don Watkins is one of today's most vocal opponents of the welfare state and coauthor, with Yaron Brook, of the national best-seller *Free Market Revolution: How Ayn Rand's Ideas Can End Big Government.*

A fellow at the Ayn Rand Institute, Don studies Social Security reform, the welfare state, and the moral foundations of capitalism. He has been interviewed on hundreds of radio and TV programs, and speaks regularly at conferences and university campuses, including Stanford, Brown, University of Virginia, and the University of Chicago, and he frequently debates supporters of the welfare state. Don is the host of a weekly podcast on the welfare state, *The Debt Dialogues.*

A Forbes.com columnist from 2010 to 2013, his writings have also appeared in *The Guardian, USA Today, Forbes, Christian Science Monitor, Investor's Business Daily, The Daily Caller,* and FoxNews.com, among many others.

You can find Don's work at www.endthedebtdraft.com and follow him on Twitter at @dwatkins3.